Slide Kitchen
Camp complete.
AF584361
ARB
4X4 ACCESSORIES

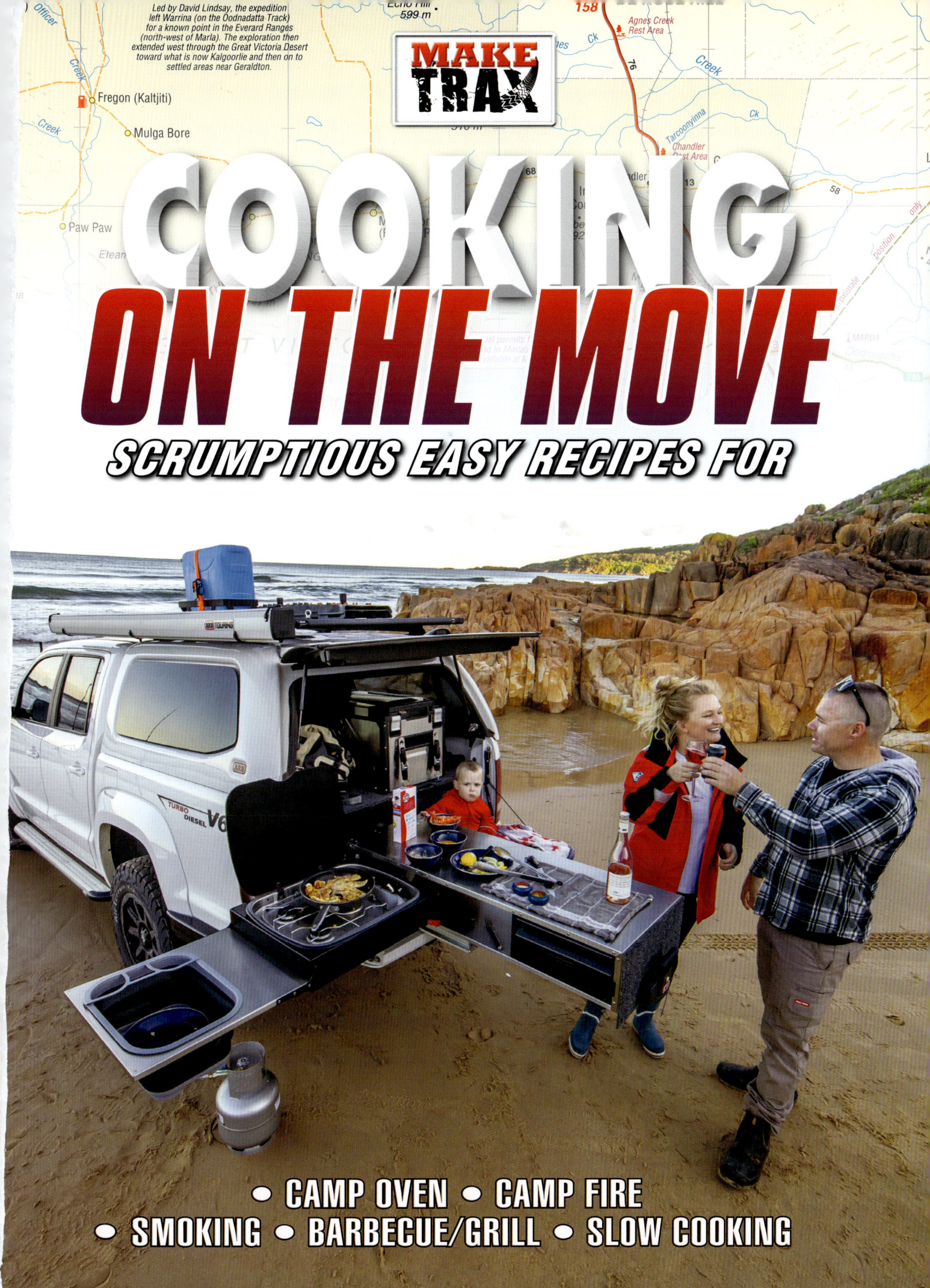
MAKE TRAX
COOKING
ON THE MOVE
SCRUMPTIOUS EASY RECIPES FOR
• CAMP OVEN • CAMP FIRE
• SMOKING • BARBECUE/GRILL • SLOW COOKING
Led by David Lindsay, the expedition left Warrina (on the Oodnadatta Track) for a known point in the Everard Ranges (north-west of Marla). The exploration then extended west through the Great Victoria Desert toward what is now Kalgoorlie and then on to settled areas near Geraldton.
Echo Hill 599 m
Fregon (Kaltjiti)
Mulga Bore
Paw Paw
Agnes Creek Rest Area
Chandler Rest Area
TURBO DIESEL V6

First published 2011
Re-printed 2015, 2021, 2023

Published and distributed by
Australian Fishing Network
PO Box 544 Croydon, Victoria 3136
Telephone: (03) 9729 8788 Facsimile: (03) 9729 7833
Email: sales@afn.com.au
Website: www.afn.com.au

ISBN: 97818651 340 24

Printed in China

COOKING ON THE MOVE

SCRUMPTIOUS EASY RECIPES FOR

• CAMP OVEN • CAMP FIRE • SMOKING
• BARBECUE/GRILL • SLOW COOKING

Contents

CADAC

Introduction

COOKING ON THE MOVE

Thousands of Australians are now on the move! A few years ago the term 'Grey Nomads' referred to the thousands of retirees that packed the 4WD, hitched the caravan or camper trailer and took off around Australia over winter.

Now it's not just retirees! The list grows and there are thousands of Aussies of all ages that have joined this way of living.

All of them have one common bond – the joy of – Cooking On the Move – every night.

Cooking On the Move is the complete cook book for those travelling around Australia whether it's for six months, four weeks, a week or just a weekend getaway. It's a cookbook that won't affect your valuable recreation time! Great recipes that look and taste delicious. They are easy to prepare and often don't require a lot of ingredients but are remarkably appetising and simply very tasty.

The team at **AFN *Outdoors*** involved some terrific partners in creating this recipe book. These included some of the best known camping and cooking accessories used by those who travel around Australia.

Dream Pot and the ***Thermos Shuttle*** are perfect slow cookers for those on the move and the recipes provided will be enjoyed by many who travel this great country.

The ***Cadac Safari*** is a unique gas griller that has 1001 uses and has to be one of the best On the Move cookers that a traveller could include in their kit.

The ***Misty Gully*** smoker exemplifies a style of cooking that is about to take off. Smoking food is generally accepted in Australia and very popular amongst anglers. But all sorts of food can be smoked and once smoked can be kept for several days in simple cooling.

Camp Oven cooking is also very popular and **Andrea Prickett** has come up with a range of recipes especially for the camp oven.

Lastly open fire, campfire, barbecue or just plain cooking on the gas stove has been catered for as well. Again **Andrea Prickett** has put together some great mouth watering recipes that will please every taste.

FIVE-IN-ONE COOKING SYSTEM

Originating in South Africa, CADAC may be the "new kid on the barbecue block" in Australia, but they bring with them 60 years of experience and dedication to versatility (for any meal), portability (to carry anywhere) and quality. It is a very durable product and performs to expectations, even in the rugged Aussie Outback!

The Cadac Safari Chef is a very versatile and unique combo-cooking system based around portable grilling in the outdoors. Remarkably, it can cook in five unique ways.

1. Fat-free barbecue – meat, vegetables.
2. Non-stick DuPont ribbed griddle plate for grilling.
3. Non-stick DuPont lipped breakfast plate.
4. Camping stove – boiling water, making sauces
5. Dome/Wok – stew, soup, stir-fries or oven

The Cadac Safari Chef can barbecue burgers and kebabs with the grated grill surface. The Cadac Safari Chef can cook perfect steaks and chicken on the Teflon coated non-stick reversible grill plate. Reverse the plate and use the skillet on the other side to fry eggs and bacon for those camping trips. Finally reverse the Cadac Safari Chef lid and you have a wok ready to go!

The Cadac Safari Chef comes with a convenient grill carrying case. It also has folding support legs. The Cadac Safari Chef is the most perfect for camping, tailgating and cooking out at home.

Other features of this remarkable cooking system include:

- Safari Chef is designed to let grease run off to prevent flare-ups when using the mini fat-free barbecue and fat-free non-stick ribbed grill.
- Non-stick cooking surfaces are easy to clean. All components are dishwasher safe.
- 7,300 BTUs For use only with a disposable 450 gm propane cylinder containing HD-5 Propane LP Gas marked in accordance with the specifications for LP gas Cylinders of the U.S. Department of Transportation (DOT 39). Cylinder is available at most grocery stores and retailers.
- Completely portable, comes with convenient carrying bag.
- Grill Dimensions: 50.9 x 38.1 x 43.2 centimetres
- Comes with a two year warranty.

SAFARI CHEF

The pick up and go anywhere, anytime, outdoor kitchen.

This compact and versatile gas BBQ offers five interchangeable cooking surfaces:

- a camping stove
- Barbeque
- non-stick reversible grill
- a lid that doubles up as a wok
- using the lid and BBQ together creates a mini oven.

Ideal for camping, hiking, fishing, caravanning and sports events.

Wok/Lid ideal for stir-fries, sauces, rice, pasta, etc, with a 3.8 litre capacity. When used as a lid it is perfect as a roasting oven.

Non-stick reversible griddle ideal for grilling meat, chicken, breakfasts, pancakes or vegetables.

Mini BBQ top ideal for fat-free barbecuing of chops, fish or vegetables.

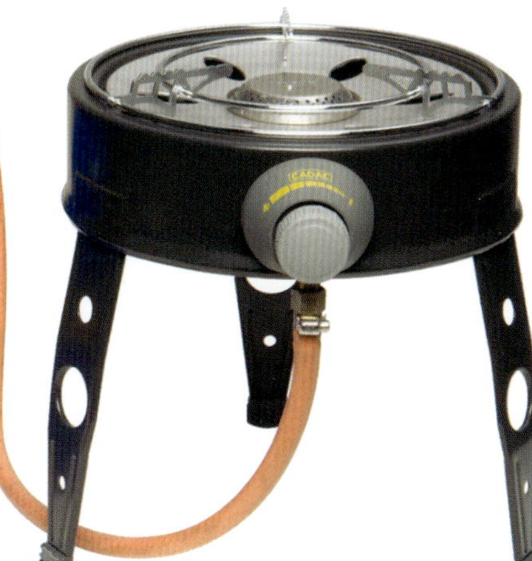

Cooker top for boiling water, brewing coffee, etc.

Fold away legs for easy storage.

SEAFOOD PAELLA

Serves 6–8

Ingredients

Assortment of seafood: langoustines, baby octopus, mussels, crabs, calamari & clams
good quality olive oil
1–2 cloves garlic, chopped
1 medium onion, finely chopped
1 cup sweet peppers (red, green and yellow), chopped
1–2 tbs ground paprika
1 bunch parsley, chopped
2–3 cups long grain or paella rice
good pinch of saffron, soaked in 80 mL hot water
1 1/2 litre fish stock
1 cup white wine

Method

1. Select the desired amount of seafood of your choice. Clean, rinse and drain thoroughly.
2. Using a paella pan or large frying pan, gently fry the chopped garlic in 4 tablespoons of oil.
3. Fry all seafood separately, and then put aside.
4. Heat the pan with 2 more tablespoons of oil. Stir in the onion, sweet peppers, paprika and half of the parsley. Add the rice and fry for a further 5 minutes, stirring constantly.
5. Pour in the saffron solution and wine. Keep turning the rice to prevent burning.
6. Add in the fish stock gradually, as the rice absorbs the liquid. When all the liquid has been absorbed, arrange the seafood on top of the rice and sprinkle the remaining amount of parsley over the dish. Serve immediately.

FUSION KEDGEREE

Serves 6–8

PREPARATION TIME: 20 MINUTES

COOKING TIME: 50 MINUTES

This is a truly fusion dish that was originally taken from India. It was then Anglicised by adding egg and haddock. I have returned it to its origin somewhat by adding other typical Asian ingredients, and retaining the Indian ones.

Ingredients

400–500 gm prawns
1/2 tbs coarse sea salt
2 tbs butter
3 tbs olive oil
1–2 cloves garlic, minced
2 cm ginger root, minced
1 cup white wine
4 cups water
10 spring onions, chopped (reserve half for garnish)
2 tsp whole cumin
1–2 cinnamon sticks, broken into small pieces
1 1/2 cups uncooked rice
1 bunch coriander, chopped
2 eggs, hard-boiled, chopped or shredded omelette
Juice of 1/2 lime or 1/4 lemon (reserve grated zest)
Salt and pepper to taste

Method

1. Make an incision along the spine of the prawns. Remove veins, sprinkle with coarse sea salt and toss. After 5 to 10 minutes, rinse under cold water until water runs clear. Drain and put aside.
2. Heat 1 tablespoon of each of the butter and oil in a wok. Add garlic and ginger. Fry these for a minute or so to release the flavours before adding the prawns. Add the wine and water, and poach the prawns lightly. Remove the prawns as soon as you see the first bubbles emerging. Reserve the liquid.
3. Place the wok back over the flame. Heat the remaining butter and oil. Lightly fry half of the spring onions, and add the spices. Finally stir in the rice, making sure that all the rice is coated evenly. Add the reserved stock 1 cup at a time; keep stirring to mix the solids and liquid. Cover and cook over low heat until the rice is fluffy. This should take at least 20-25 minutes.
4. Remove from the heat. Using a wooden spoon, gently stir in the coriander, remaining spring onions, egg, lemon/lime juice and zest. Add salt and pepper to suit your taste. Lastly, arrange the prawns over the rice.

SEARED TUNA
ON SALAD NEST

PREPARATION TIME: 10 MINUTES

COOKING TIME: 5 MINUTES

Ingredients

600–800 gm tuna fillet
4 tbs olive oil
4 tbs coriander and /or basil pesto
Juice of a lemon
2 tbs soy sauce
Salt and pepper
Pinch of sugar
Salad leaves
2 Roasted peppers
1/2 cucumber, sliced diagonally
Sprouts
Avocado pear (optional), stoned and sliced lengthways

Method

1. Slice tuna into 2 cm thick slices. Rub half of olive oil into tuna.
2. Heat 'Ribbed Grill' until very hot. Place tuna on grill, and cook for 2–3 minutes on each side.
3. Remove tuna and cut into 1 cm strips.
4. In a bowl combine the tuna, remaining oil, pesto, lemon juice, soy sauce, salt, pepper and sugar. Toss well.
5. Arrange salad leaves and the rest of the prepared ingredients on a platter. Place tuna with marinade over the salad and serve at once. It is irresistable with a loaf of the finest!

SPICY SNAPPER FRITTATA

Serves 4–6

PREPARATION TIME: 10 MINUTES

COOKING TIME: 10 MINUTES

Ingredients

- 200–300 gm snapper fillets, or white fish sliced
- 1/2 red onion, cut into rings
- 1/4 each of green, yellow and red pepper, shredded
- 8 eggs, lightly beaten
- Salt and freshly ground pepper
- 1/4 tsp cumin
- 1/4 tsp cayenne pepper
- 1/4 tsp ground ginger
- 1/4 tsp cinnamon
- 3 tsp olive oil
- 1–2 sprigs of spring onion, chopped
- 10 slices of French bread

Method

1. Heat a pan or Paella Pan and coat with 2 tablespoons of olive oil when hot. Gently fry the onion and peppers. Add salt, black pepper and spices.
2. Pour the remaining tablespoon of olive oil around the edge of the pan. Arrange the bread slices around the edge, slightly overlapping each other. This will form a 'retaining wall' preventing the egg mixture from spreading.
3. Pour the egg mixture in the centre and reduce the heat to its lowest, then add the sliced haddock. Cover with a lid. It will take approximately 5 minutes for all of the egg mixture to set.
4. Finally garnish with the chopped spring onions. Cut into wedges and serve.

CRUSTY FISH CUTLETS
WITH SPICY HERBS

Serves 4

PREPARATION TIME: 10 MINUTES

COOKING TIME: 10 MINUTES

Ingredients

4 fish cutlets, washed and dried with paper towel. Any white fish cutlet can be used in this recipe: cod, whiting, kingfish...

Juice and zest of a lemon

1 tsp sugar

2 tsp salt

2 cloves garlic, sliced

1 green chilli, seeded and chopped

1–2 tbs oil

For a few taste diversions, choose one of the following herbs and add to the seasoning: dill, basil, parsley, rocket, coriander. Ginger can also be added.

Method

1. Marinate the fish in all ingredients listed for at least 1 hour.
2. Heat and coat the grill with oil. Fry fish for 5 minutes on each side until crusty and golden.
3. Garnish with herb sprigs and serve. Drizzle more oil over before serving.

NOTE:

Use only one herb at a time as some are too strong to be combined.

Fish, to taste right, must swim three times
—in water, in butter, and in wine.

POLISH PROVERB

SEAFOOD POTJIE

Serves 6–8

PREPARATION TIME: 10 MINUTES

COOKING TIME: 25 MINUTES

Ingredients

- 4 fillets of white fish
- 4 medium calamari tubes
- 4 fillet of gummy shark
- 1 kg mussels, cleaned and de-bearded
- 1 red onion, chopped
- 2 heads of fennel, sliced, reserving the tops
- 1/2 cup olive oil
- Garlic, minced
- 5 medium potatoes or sweet potatoes, cut into big chunks
- 1/4 cup fish stock,
- 1/4 cup white wine
- 2 tbs flat-leaf parsley, chopped
- 1–1 1/2 cup fresh cream
- Salt and pepper to taste

Method

1. Clean all fish thoroughly. Cut them into big chunks.
2. In the potjie pot, fry the fennels and onion until transparent. Remove from the potjie and set aside. Repeat the same process for the potatoes.
3. Heat up the potjie again until red hot, then fry the white fish with minced garlic for a minute and layer the other fish alternating with fennel tops. Add the potatoes in the next layer. Reserve the mussels, onion and fennel for the final layer to be added at a later stage. Pour the fish stock and wine. Cover and cook for another 5 minutes or until all shells are opened.
4. Empty the potjie contents into a serving bowl. Remove the stalks of the fennel tops. Pour fresh cream evenly over and sprinkle with chopped parsley. Season with salt and pepper and serve immediately.
5. Any combination of fish makes excellent substitutes. The importance lies in quick cooking, so as not to turn the fish into mush and the calamari into rubbery tubes! The Green Rub can also be used with this dish.
6. A garlic mayonnaise is a fantastic companion for this dish.

ROAST CHICKEN WITH VEGETABLES

Serves: 4–6

PREPARATION TIME: 10 MINUTES

COOKING TIME: 70 MINUTES

Ingredients

- 1 whole chicken, no more than 1.5 kg
- 1 pinch of sugar
- 2 tbs salt
- 1 tsp coarsely ground black pepper
- 2 tbs lemon juice, optional
- 1 tbsp each: thyme, rosemary, sage, finely chopped
- 1 cup of water for gravy
- 1 kg pumpkin, cut into 2 cm thick pieces
- Sprinkle of cinnamon
- 1 kg potatoes, sliced into 1 cm thick discs
- Salt and pepper to taste
- 1 tbs oil

Method

1. Wash and dry the chicken. Mix half of the salt and pepper and all of the sugar, lemon juice and chopped herbs together. Rub this mixture into the skin and cavity of the chicken. Set aside for as long as possible.
2. Toss the pumpkin with some of the remaining salt and cinnamon. Season the potatoes with the balance of the salt and pepper.
3. Heat up the roasting dish on high heat for about 5 minutes. Brush the surface with oil.
4. Place the chicken breast-side down in the centre of the dish. Add the potatoes on the edge around the chicken. Cover with the lid. Turn the heat down to medium and roast for 20 minutes.
5. Turn the chicken breast-side up and place the pumpkin pieces among the potatoes. Carry on roasting for another 40 minutes, or until the liquid runs clear when inserting a skewer into the thickest part of the breast. Turn the vegetables from time to time to prevent the pumpkin from burning.
6. Lift the chicken and vegetables out of the dish while you make the gravy. Pour the cup of water into the roasting dish. Scrape the pan a little to lift all the meats' juices from the pan. Reduce until liquid has halved. Strain and serve with the chicken.
7. *NOTE:* Other vegetables such as zucchini and carrots can be added in towards the end.

CHICKEN BAKE

Serves: 4–5

PREPARATION TIME: 5 MINUTES

COOKING TIME: 15 MINUTES

Ingredients

8 – 10 chicken portions on bone, preferably thighs and drumsticks
4 tbs mayonnaise
4 tbs tomato sauce
Salt and pepper to taste

Method

1. Clean and pat-dry the chicken pieces. Rub with salt and coarsely ground pepper.
2. In a bowl, combine the mayonnaise and tomato sauce and mix well. Coat each piece of chicken evenly with the mixture.
3. Place chicken pieces over a medium heated surface. Cover with lid and bake until the chicken is cooked.

   It should take approximately 12–15 minutes.

SIMMERED CHICKEN IN GREEN COCONUT CURRY

Serves 4

PREPARATION TIME: 40 MINUTES

COOKING TIME: 15 MINUTES

Ingredients

- 1 tbs soy sauce
- 1/4 tsp sugar
- 1/2 tsp salt
- 1/2 tbs corn flour
- 2 tbs water
- 400 gm chicken breasts, sliced thinly
- 2 tbs oil
- 1/2 tbs green curry paste
- 2 cups assorted vegetables, shredded or sliced
- 1 clove garlic, minced
- 400 mL coconut milk
- 1–2 tbs fish sauce
- Handful of basil or coriander leaves

Method

1. Combine the chicken with the first 5 ingredients, mix thoroughly and set aside for at least half an hour.
2. Heat the wok, add oil, garlic and green curry paste, then the chicken. Cook for 2–3 minutes until the chicken has browned evenly. Stir occasionally.
3. Add coconut milk and fish sauce. Turn the heat down, and simmer for another 3–4 minutes until the chicken is tender and the sauce has reduced. The shredded vegetables should be added half way during simmering.
4. Garnish with basil or coriander leaves. Serve with hot crusty bread or any accompaniment of your choice.

CHICKEN TAGINE

Serves 4

Ingredients

- 400 gm chicken thigh or breast, cut into cubes
- 1 clove garlic, minced
- 1 tbs harrissa paste
- 1 bunch flat-leaf parsley, roughly chop the stalks and finely chop the leaves
- 1 tsp cumin seeds, whole or ground
- 1 tsp fennel seeds, whole or ground
- 1 stick cinnamon
- Preserved lemon, if available, otherwise use 2 thick slices of lemon, salted on both sides and leave for at least 30 minutes to 1 hour
- 10 dried apricot halves, cut into quarters
- 10 dried peach halves, optional, cut into quarters
- Salt and pepper to taste
- 2 tbs oil
- 1/4 cup water

Method

1. Combine chicken, garlic, parsley stalks and harrisa paste, mix well and put aside.
2. Heat pan, add oil, cumin seeds and cinnamon stick. When the seeds start popping, add the chicken.
3. Turn the chicken over once or twice before adding water. Cover and cook for 5 minutes or until the chicken is 70% cooked.
4. Add the remaining ingredients except the parsley leaves, stir a few times, cover and cook for a further 2–5 minutes.
5. Transfer to a serving dish. Sprinkle the chopped parsley leaves over the dish. Season with salt and pepper and serve immediately.

TURKEY WITH CRANBERRY STUFFING

Serves 4

Ingredients

2–3 large turkey legs or 4 turkey breasts
1/4 cup oil

STUFFING:

1/4 cup cranberries
4 tbs Verjuice or grape juice
2 tbs roasted pine-nuts or almonds
2 tbs parsley, finely chopped
1 egg
3 tbs bread crumbs
3 tbs grated parmesan cheese
Salt and pepper to taste

Method

1. Combine all the stuffing ingredients and set aside for 1 hour.
2. If using legs:

   Loosen the skin around the leg. Stuff each leg until all the stuffing has been used up.

   Brush oil over the legs. Grill for 20 minutes until the skin is golden and translucent. Pierce the thickest part of the meat with a metal skewer. When the juice runs clear, the legs are done.
3. If using breasts:

   Use a rolling pin to flatten the breasts to equal thickness. Divide the stuffing into 4 portions. Place the stuffing at one end of the breast and roll up the breast to form a roulade. You can secure the breast roll with string or a tooth pick. Fry the rolls in oil over high heat for 5 minutes to seal the meat. Then turn the heat down to medium or low and cook until the juice runs clear when pierced with a skewer.

TURKEY POTJIE

Serves 4–6

PREPARATION TIME: 10 MINUTES

COOKING TIME: 45 MINUTES

Ingredients

- 1 1/2–2 kg turkey breasts or thighs
- 2 onions, chopped
- 3 cloves garlic, sliced
- 1 whole cinnamon stick
- 4 cloves
- 1/4 cup oil
- 1/2 cup dry white wine
- 1 cup baby potatoes
- 1 handful of parsley
- 1 cup carrots
- 1 cup cabbage or spinach
- Salt and pepper to taste

Method

1. Cut meat into 5 to 7 cm chunks. Place potjie pot* over high heat. Pour in half of the oil, fry the onions, garlic, cinnamon and cloves to release the fragrance.
2. Brown the meat a few pieces at a time, otherwise the juice from the meat will make it too soupy. Remove the meat and set it aside once you have browned all the pieces of meat evenly.
3. Pour the remaining oil into the pot. When it is hot, line the bottom with the baby potatoes, then parsley, carrots, browned meat, and lastly the leafy greens and the wine.
4. Season each layer of ingredients to your liking. Turn the heat down to medium and cook for 20 to 30 minutes.
5. Serve hot with any one of the salsas in this cook book.

*Alternatively, use a deep cast-iron casserole dish.

PORK FILLET
WITH APPLE STUFFING

Serves 4–6

PREPARATION TIME: 10 MINUTES

COOKING TIME: 25 MINUTES

Ingredients

2 medium sized pork fillets
250 gm packet of streaky bacon
1 small cooking apple, peeled and cored
Juice and zest of 1/2 a lemon
50 gm chorico sausage slices
1/2 tbs honey
1 tbs soy sauce
1/2 tbs brandy or dry sherry
Salt and black pepper to taste
A handful of sage leaves

Method

1. Cut the apple into quarters and slice thinly. Toss with lemon juice and zest.
2. Slit the pork fillets lengthwise. Rub honey, soy sauce and brandy or sherry into the fillets.
3. Place half of the apple and chorico slices, plus a few sage leaves into the first fillet. Season with salt and pepper.
4. Wrap half of the bacon strips around the fillet securing the stuffing. Repeat for the other fillet with the remaining stuffing.
5. Brown the two fillets evenly for 5 minutes over high heat. Then turn the heat down to medium and cook for a further 8–10 minutes.
6. If you have a lid, turn the heat off and leave the fillets under the lid for a further 10 minutes. Otherwise wrap the fillets in tin foil and let them rest for 10 minutes before serving.
7. Cut the fillet into 2–4cm slices. Any of the Salsas on pages 55–56 and Grilled Polenta on page 51 make excellent companions to this dish.

STICKY RIBS

Serves 2–4

Ingredients

500 gm–1 kg pork, beef or lamb ribs
1 cup Secret Marinade (refer to recipes under sauces on pg 60)
Rosemary or any of the more hardy herbs
Salt and pepper to taste

Method

1. Marinate the ribs in the sauce for an hour or overnight. Add more salt and pepper if needed.
2. The longer the ribs have been marinated, the better the result.
3. Pre-heat the grill or a pan on high heat.
4. Place the ribs on the grill and turn heat down to low.
5. Cook with the lid on for 15 minutes, turning once or twice.
6. Uncover the lid, cook until the ribs look crispy and the sauce glistens.

PORK CHOPS
IN PINEAPPLE & GINGER SAUCE

Serves 3–6

PREPARATION TIME: 5 MINUTES

COOKING TIME: 25 MINUTES

Ingredients

6 pork loin chops, each about 2–3 cm thick
1 tbs oil
Salt and pepper to taste
1 medium pineapple, peeled and sliced
3 slices fresh root ginger
1 clove garlic
1 tsp sugar
1/4 cup red or white wine

Method

1. Heat a grill over high heat. Brush the surface with a little oil and fry the pork chops for 3–5 minutes on either side. Season with salt and pepper. The cooking time depends on the thickness of the meat as well as your preference.
2. While the meat is cooking, blend half of the pineapple slices along with the garlic and ginger. Add a little water if necessary. Set aside.
3. Once the chops are done to your liking, lift the meat onto a serving platter or individual plates. Place the balance of the pineapple slices onto the pan. Pour the wine over the pan and the mixture will bubble and reduce to a slightly thicker sauce. Add the blended mixture, sugar and a little more wine or water. Reduce the sauce further. When it reaches the consistency of thin syrup, remove it from the heat. Pour over the chops and serve immediately.
4. Apricot is also very compatible with pork, but leave out the ginger if you use apricot instead of pineapple!

SHORT RIBS IN COLA

Serves 4

PREPARATION TIME: 10 MINUTES

COOKING TIME: 15 MINUTES

Ingredients

- 1–1 1/2 kg of short ribs, cut into strips
- 5 cm fresh root ginger, sliced
- 4 cloves garlic, sliced
- 1 ripe tomato, roughly chopped
- 1 tbs oil
- 1 cup cola
- 2 tbs spicy chutney or barbecue sauce on page 62
- 2 tbs brandy or sherry
- Salt and pepper to taste

Method

1. Crush ginger, garlic, tomato and oil in a pestle and mortar to form a paste. Add the paste to the rest of the ingredients and marinate the ribs overnight.
2. Light the grill or coals. Barbeque the ribs over medium heat for 10–15 minutes, basting all the while with the marinade. Turn the heat down if the marinade starts to burn.
3. Wrap half of each rib with tin foil to create tasty finger foods for picnics and beach parties.

VENISON SAUSAGE

Serves 4–6

PREPARATION TIME: 10 MINUTES

COOKING TIME: 30 MINUTES

Ingredients

1–2 kg venison sausages
100 gm fatty bacon, optional
1 small onion, chopped
2–3 tomatoes, chopped
2 cloves garlic, chopped
1 1/2 cups pre-cooked lentils
1 tsp sugar
1 1/2 tsp salt
A handful of fresh parsley or coriander

Method

1. In this day and age, we no longer have the time to make our own sausages. Venison meats are widely available now in most reputable butcheries and that's where you can ask your butcher to make you some juicy venison sausages.
2. Fry the sausages in fatty bacon until golden brown. Remove the sausages from the pan. Sauté the onion and garlic until soft and add in the chopped tomatoes. Season with sugar and salt.
3. Cover and simmer over a low heat until the ingredients turn into a sauce.
4. Return the sausages to the pan along with the lentils. Cook further until the sausages are cooked through.
5. Throw in the chopped herbs and serve immediately.

VENISON SADDLE

Serves 6–8

PREPARATION TIME: 5 MINUTES + MARINATING TIME

COOKING TIME: 1-1½ HOURS

Ingredients

1–2 kg of venison saddle
1 cup red wine
2 sprigs rosemary
1 portion of Five Fragrant Spice Rub on page 59
4 tbs honey or apricot jam
Juice of 1 lemon

Method

1. Combine all ingredients and marinate the saddle for 2–3 days or at least overnight.
2. Set the grill at 200°C.
3. Secure the saddle on the rotisserie and cook for 20 minutes. Keep basting all the time. Then reduce the heat to 175 C° and cook for another 40 minutes. Let the saddle rest for 5–10 minutes before serving.

NOTE:

Add ½ hour for every kilogram of meat for rare and ¾ hour per kilogram for medium to well done meat.

Reduce the apricot glaze on page 61 to serve as a relish. They are a match made in heaven!

VENISON SHREDS

Serves 4–6

PREPARATION TIME: 15 MINUTES + MARINATING TIME

COOKING TIME: 60 MINUTES

Ingredients

1–2 kg of venison steak
1/4 cup bacon fat, or 4 tbs olive oil
1 medium paprika, julienne
1 chilli, shredded, optional
1 small red onion, thinly sliced
1/2 cup black olives
1/4 cup tomato flesh, julienne
2 tbs parsley leaves, roughly torn by hand

MARINADE

1/2 cup red wine
1 lemon, juiced
1 bay leaf
5 black or green pepper corns
1 tbs corn flour, optional
2 tbs oil
1 tbs honey
2 tbs raisins or sultanas
Salt and pepper to taste

Method

1. Combine all marinade ingredients together and marinate the meat overnight at the least. The longer the marinating period the better the result. Turn the meat over a few times during the marinating
2. Use ½ of the fat or oil to flash-fry the onion and paprika. Remove and reserve.
3. Add the balance of the fat or oil into the pan. Brown the meat thoroughly over high heat. Pour in the marinade and simmer over medium heat for 20–30 minutes or until the meat is tender.
4. Strain the meat and let it cool down enough to shred the meat by hand (the texture of hand torn meat is much smoother than cutting with a knife).
5. Heat up the sauce again over high heat and reduce it further to form a syrupy sauce.
6. Toss the meat, olives, tomatoes, chillies (if using), parsley, onion and paprika into the hot sauce if you desire a warm dish. Otherwise, let the sauce cool down for a cool summer dish.
7. This is also an excellent filling for wraps and spuds.

FRUITY VENISON STEW

Serves 4–6

PREPARATION TIME: 10 MINUTES

COOKING TIME: 55 MINUTES

Ingredients

800 gm–1 kg venison meat, cut into 5 cm chunks
1–2 onions, chopped
3 cloves garlic, sliced
1/2 cup red wine
3 cooking apples, each cut into 6 pieces
1/2 cup parsley
2 sprigs oregano
1 cup cherry tomatoes, halved
8–10 prunes
Salt and pepper to taste
Oil for cooking

Method

1. Brown the meat on both sides evenly. Add the onions and garlic and fry for a minute or two.
2. Now add the parsley and oregano, give it a few stirs and add the rest of the ingredients. Bring to the boil, turn the heat down and allow to simmer for 30-45 minutes until the meat is tender.
3. Stir from time to time to make sure the apples and fruits are not being trapped at the bottom. You may need to add a little water as well.

VARIATIONS:

Ostrich, turkey or pork are fantastic substitutes.

Add in a portion of Sweet Spicy Tomato Sauce (page 62) to make a saucier dish.

The Secret Marinade on page 60 is a great tenderiser of meat. Marinate the meat overnight if possible.

BEEF FILLET OR RUMP
STIR FRY

Serves 4

PREPARATION TIME: 10 MINUTES

COOKING TIME: 10 MINUTES

Ingredients

400–600 gm beef fillet or rump steaks
6 spring onions
1/2 white onion and 1/2 red onion
1 tbs coriander seeds, finely ground
Salt and pepper to taste
Oil
Splash of Soy sauce or oyster sauce, optional
Or even the BBQ sauce (refer recipe on page 62)

Method

1. The steaks can be left whole or cut into 1cm thick strips. Rub all dry spices into meat, leave aside for at least 30 minutes.
2. Cut spring onions into 5cm long strips and cut the onions into segments.
3. Heat the pan until red hot. Add oil and meat immediately and cook for 3 minutes on each side, depending on how you like your meat done. Stir with a spatula from time to time.
4. Add the spring onions around the edge of the meat, and cook further for a minute or two.
5. Turn the heat off. Add more salt and pepper to taste or splash the sauces over the meat.

SPICY BEEF BURGER PATTIES

Serves 4

PREPARATION TIME: 10 MINUTES

COOKING TIME: 10 MINUTES

Ingredients

500–600 gm beef, minced
1 egg
2 tbs flat leaf parsley, roughly crushed
1 tbs sage
1 sprig thyme
1 sprig rosemary
3 tsp salt
1 tsp ground pepper
1 tbs ground cumin
1/2 tbs ground cloves
1 tbs coriander seeds
1 medium red onion, finely chopped
4 tbs olive oil
4 burger buns

Method

1. Finely chop all herbs. Mix all the ingredients together except olive oil and the buns. Mix well.
2. Leave aside to stand or refrigerate overnight.
3. Place the grilling pan over high heat.
4. Shape the meat mixture into four burger patties. Brush one side of the patties with oil. Place the oiled side down onto the grilling pan and cook over medium heat for 3–5 minutes.
5. Brush with more olive oil before turning over. Cook for another 3–5 minutes.
6. Place the patties in the buns and serve immediately with your choice of condiments or a green salad.
7. Any other minced meat or fish make excellent substitutes.

BEEF FILLET WITH FIERY SAUCE

Serves 4–6

PREPARATION TIME: 10 MINUTES

COOKING TIME: 45 MINUTES

Ingredients

1 medium to large beef fillet
3 tbs coarsely ground black pepper
1 tbs coarse sea salt
2 tbs coarsely ground coriander seeds

SAUCE

1 green chilli, sliced
1 red chilli, sliced
4 tbs oil
3 tbs soy sauce
2 tbs brandy or dry sherry
1 tsp honey or sugar
4 tbs lemon juice
1 tsp cumin, optional

Method

1. Mix salt, pepper and coriander seeds and coat the length of the fillet evenly.
2. Combine all sauce ingredients and bring them to the boil in a saucepan then simmer to reduce and thicken the sauce. Reserve the sauce for the final stage.
3. Grill the fillet over high heat (coal or gas) for 15–25 minutes. Make sure that you rotate the sides to cook the fillet evenly.
4. Remove and let the fillet rest in a covered dish or wrap it up in tin foil for a further 5–10 minutes.
5. Slice the fillet and arrange it on a platter before pouring the sauce over.
6. You can garnish the fillet with some chilli shreds or rings.

BALSAMIC BEEF IN TORTILLA WRAPS

Serves 6

PREPARATION TIME: 5 MINUTES

COOKING TIME: 15 MINUTES

Ingredients

12 tortilla wraps (available from most local supermarkets)
600–900 gm beef fillet or rump, cut into 10 cm sections
1 tbs crushed black peppercorns
2 tbs olive oil
10 sage leaves, torn into small pieces
2 tbs soy sauce
2 tbs balsamic vinegar
1 tbs salt
Lettuce leaves, sprouts and watercress
Plus any additional salad ingredients to your liking: (Leaves can be served whole. Carrots and cucumbers should be shredded).

Method

1. Rub crushed peppercorns, sage leaves and some olive oil into the beef. Set aside.
2. Turn the grill onto high heat. Place meat sections on the very hot grill and grill for 5 minutes on each side. Remove and wrap in foil.
3. While the meat is resting, warm the tortilla wraps individually over medium to low heat on a flat pan. Keep them warm in foil once they have all been cooked.
4. Unwrap the fillet and slice, against the grain, then cut into thin strips. Toss the meat with soy sauce, vinegar and salt. Wrap the strips of beef and leaves, plus desired ingredients, in tortilla.
5. Suggestions for other ingredients: avocado pear, bell peppers, rocket, coriander, mint, re-hydrated mung bean noodles, omelette strips and assorted cheeses.

LAMB
WITH LEMON & MINT

Serves 3 (If using loin chops.)

Serves 6 (If using de-boned leg of lamb.)

PREPARATION TIME: 5 MINUTES

COOKING TIME: 15-20 MINUTES

Ingredients

6 loin lamb chops
1/4 salted preserved lemon
A handful of mint
1 tsp ground cardamom
A pinch of sugar
1 tbs olive oil
A dash of sherry, brandy or even mirin (cooking saki)

Method

1. Combine all the ingredients. Rub the marinade really well into the meat, cover and set aside. As always it is best to marinate the meat overnight. Otherwise marinate at least 30 minutes before cooking.
2. You can cook this dish with a variety of CADAC surfaces:

a. Charcoal kettle: moderate coals/heat for 15–20 minutes depending on your preference.

b. Carri Chef: you can use the ribbed or flat grill over moderate heat for 15–25 minutes.

c. Any of the CADAC gas BBQs.

d. You can use the lid with any of these (above-mentioned) styles of cooking, which creates a convection oven. This reduces the cooking time to about 20 minutes.

e. Add an extra 10 minutes if you are using a de-boned leg of lamb.

ROAST FILLET OF LAMB SALAD

Serves 6–8

PREPARATION TIME: 10 MINUTES

COOKING TIME: 10 MINUTES

Ingredients

600–800 gm loin fillets of lamb
1 large clove garlic, chopped
A handful of fresh mint, chopped
1–2 tsp ground cinnamon
1–2 tsp ground cumin
1–2 tsp cayenne pepper
1 sprig rosemary, chopped
2 tbs lemon juice
Salt and black pepper to taste
4 tbs olive oil
Salad leaves and blanched asparagus

Method

1. Coat the lamb fillets well with all ingredients except oil, salad leaves and asparagus. Set aside for at least 10 minutes.
2. Heat a pan over high heat. Fry the fillets in oil for 4–5 minutes. Remove and rest the meat until ready to use.
3. Slice the fillets into thin strips. Toss with salad leaves and asparagus.
4. Season with more salt and pepper and add more mint leaves to make a minty salad.

BUTTERFLIED LEG OF LAMB

Serves 6–8

Ingredients

$1\frac{1}{2}$–2 kg leg of lamb, butterflied
200 mL buttermilk
2 portions of Worldly Rub (see page 58)
Oil

Method

1. Combine buttermilk and World Rub to form a marinade for the lamb. For the best result, marinate overnight. Otherwise, marinade the meat for at least 3–4 hours.
2. Brush the kettle grill with oil. Cook the lamb over medium coals for 30–40 minutes depending on your preference.
3. Remove and set aside for 5–10 minutes.
4. Slice and serve with a green salad of your choice or Corn Salsa (page 55).

MOROCCAN LAMB

Serves 6–8

Ingredients

2 kg leg of lamb, with the skin and fat trimmed off
2 cloves of garlic, slivered
Half of a pickled lemon, cut into strips
Juice of half a lemon
3 tbs sunflower oil
1 tbs dried coriander seeds
3 tsp ground cinnamon
1 tsp ground ginger
1/2 tsp ground cloves
2 tbs finely chopped fresh mint
Salt and black pepper to taste
Sprigs of rosemary, optional

Method

1. Make deep incisions all over the lamb and push garlic slivers, pickled lemon and rosemary sprigs (if using) into the cuts. Combine remaining ingredients and rub half of the mixture onto the lamb. Place lamb in large shallow dish, cover and refrigerate for 12–24 hours.
2. Preheat the BBQ over medium heat. Place the lamb on the lightly oiled grid. Cover with the lid and roast for half an hour over moderate heat.
3. Spread the remaining mixture over the lamb, cover and continue roasting for a further half an hour, or until the lamb is cooked to your liking. Allow the roast to stand for a minimum of 10 minutes before carving.

NOTE:

Basting during the roasting should be done as quickly as possible to minimise heat loss. For extra flavour and aroma, scatter a few whole cinnamon sticks and bay leaves around the BBQ when cooking the lamb.

MINTY GROUND LAMB ON SKEWER

Serves 4–6

Ingredients

400 gm ground lamb
Small onion, grated
A handful of fresh mint leaves, roughly chopped
2 lime zests
Small sprig of fresh rosemary
1 egg
1 tbs corn starch
Salt and pepper to taste
4–5 tbs water
Thick wooden skewers, soaked in cold water
A little oil for brushing the grill

Method

1. Place all ingredients into a large mixing bowl. Use a spoon or spatula to blend thoroughly. With your hands scoop up as much meat mixture as possible, smacking hard, back into the bowl.
2. Repeat for 10 minutes until you can scoop up all the mixture into a ball. The smacking action brings out natural glue in all meat and fish and it also improves the texture of the ground meat.
3. Divide the meat mixture equally to the number of wooden skewers. Pack the meat firmly around the skewers.
4. Heat up the grill on high, brush with oil, then place skewers on the grill and turn heat down to medium. Cook for 5–10 minutes each side, with or without lid.

SAUSAGES STUFFED WITH SEASONAL FRUITS

Serves 4

Ingredients

4–8 banger sized sausages (large)
4–8 pieces streaky bacon
Any seasonal fruits such as green mangos, apricots, pineapples or pears
Alternatively, dried fruits such as mangos, dates or prunes

Method

1. Make an incision down the length of the sausages. Take care not to cut all the way through.
2. Cut the fruit into smaller pieces or strips. Fill the sausages with fruit pieces and finish off by wrapping the bacon strips around the sausages. Tooth picks can be used to secure the bacon.
3. Heat the grill over medium heat. When hot, place the sausages onto the grill. Turn the sausages over occasionally to get an even golden grilled look. 15–20 minutes is sufficient for the bangers to cook through.
4. You can use cocktail sausages for a starter or a pre-meal nibble. This will take approximately 12 minutes.

MEDITERRANEAN STEW

Serves 6–8

Ingredients

- 1 cup chickpeas
- 2 chorizo sausages, sliced into 5 mm thick rounds
- 2 cups root vegetables (butternuts, pumpkins...), cubed
- 1 cup sweet potatoes, cubed
- 1 cup whole cherry tomatoes
- 1/2 cup celery, chopped
- 1/2 cup onions, chopped
- 4 cups stock (meat or vegetable), more if needed
- 2 cloves garlic, finely chopped
- 1 tsp each of cinnamon, ginger, paprika and tumeric
- Olive oil
- Salt and pepper
- Flat-leafed parsley and lemon zest, quantity to your liking

Method

1. Soak chickpeas in 3 cups of boiling water overnight. Drain and reserve.
2. Using a deep frying pan or paella pan, fry the sausage slices in a little oil until crispy. Remove sausage crisps from the pan.
3. In the same pan, add 2 more tablespoons of oil and fry onions, celery, garlic, and all ground spices. Stir to release the aroma of the spices, add the cubed vegetables one at a time, followed by the chickpeas and cherry tomatoes. Stir slowly to prevent burning and sticking. Pour in the stock and simmer slowly until all ingredients are tender and the stock thickens to a rich creamy sauce. Season with salt and pepper.
4. Serve with chopped parsley and lemon zest. Add a handfull of olives to create a richer Mediterranean colour.

One cannot think well, love well, sleep well,
if one has not dined well.

VIRGINIA WOOLF

CARAMELISED PINEAPPLE AND TROPICAL FRUITS

Serves 4

PREPARATION TIME: 5 MINUTES

COOKING TIME: 5 MINUTES

Ingredients

- 8 slices fresh pineapple, cut lengthwise
- 2–3 tsp butter
- 1 tbs sugar
- 1 stalk lemon grass, minced (optional)
- 4 nectarines, halved (or any seasonal fruit)
- Zest of 1 orange and lime
- Mascarpone cheese or whipped cream

Method

1. Heat the grill until it starts to smoke. Smear half of the butter over the fruits, place them onto the hot grill for 1–2 minutes on each side. Remove from the grill.
2. Heat the remaining butter in a pan. Add sugar, zest and lemon grass.
3. Toss in the grilled fruits, ensuring that all the pieces of fruits are well coated with the caramel.
4. Arrange on a platter and serve with mascarpone cheese or whipped cream.

SAFARI CRÈME BRÛLÉE

Serves 4

PREPARATION TIME: 5 MINUTES
COOKING TIME: 5 MINUTES

Ingredients

- 4 eggs
- 4 tsp sugar
- Vinegar, a drop or two per bowl
- 3/4 cup milk
- Rose water

Method

Combine eggs, milk and sugar in a mixing bowl. Beat well. Divide the mixture into 4 small dessert bowls. Add a drop or two of vinegar and rose water into each bowl.

Place a shallow layer of water in a wok or pan and bring to the boil. Place the bowls in the boiling water and cover with a lid. Steam for 5 minutes until the custard is set. Remove the bowls from the wok or pan and serve with a few sugar-dusted rose petals to create an exotic effect.

NOTE:
This brûleé can be served chilled.

CHOCOLATE BANANAS

Serves 6

PREPARATION TIME: 5 MINUTES
COOKING TIME: 8 MINUTES

Ingredients

- 6 bananas, skin must still be green
- 30 dark chocolate buttons
- Foil
- Dark rum

Method

Run a knife down the length of each banana. Make 5 incisions across the banana. Insert the chocolate buttons into the slits.
Wrap up each fruit in foil to look like a Christmas cracker. Place directly on the coals and leave for 5-8 minutes, depending on how soft you'd like the dessert. Open the foils, splash on the rum and serve.

A spicy cardamom syrup makes a non-alcoholic alternative to the rum.

HONEYED PEAR WITH BRIE AND PANETTONE

Serves 6

PREPARATION TIME: 5-10 MINUTES
COOKING TIME: 8 MINUTES

Ingredients

- 6 slices of panettone
- 3 large pears, cored and cut into wedges
- 1 tbs butter
- 2 tbs honey
- 2 tbs almond flakes
- 1 small round of brie cheese, cut into 6 wedges
- Icing sugar for dusting

Method

1. Lightly dry-toast the panettone in a pan. Repeat the process for the almond flakes. Set aside.
2. Heat the pan with butter. When bubbling, pour the honey over. Add the pears in just before the honey turns brown. Toss the pan to coat the pear wedges evenly and cook for 2-3 minutes. Place the brie cheese on the outskirts of the pan to warm slightly.
3. Place the panettone toast onto individual plates, divide the pears equally over the portions, add cheese on top and sprinkle over the almond flakes.
4. For the indulgent ones: finish the dish with a splash of dessert wine.

GRILLED MANGO WITH GINGER FROZEN YOGHURT

Serves 4–6

PREPARATION TIME: 45 MINUTES

COOKING TIME: 2-5 MINUTES + FREEZE OVERNIGHT

Ingredients

2–3 large, firm, but ripe mangoes
Icing sugar for dusting
2 cups natural or vanilla yoghurt
2 vanilla pods
2 tbs brandy or Verjuice (available at most Delis)
3 tbs chopped preserved ginger stems
2 tbs honey, optional

Method

1. Score the vanilla pod length-wise. Scrape the centre of the pod to get out all the seeds. Infuse the vanilla seeds in brandy or Verjuice for ½ hour.
2. Empty the yoghurt into a freezer-proof container. Stir in the vanilla infusion and the ginger stems. Taste and add honey if preferred.
3. Leave it to freeze for 1 hour. Use a fork to break up any icy bits. Repeat a couple more times and freeze until completely frozen.
4. Cut each mango into two halves. Dust with icing sugar.
5. Heat grill on high heat. Grill the flat part with butter for a couple of minutes.
6. Cut each mango half into two and serve with ginger yoghurt.

POLENTA

Ingredients

- 180 gm instant polenta
- 4 cups water
- 2 tsp salt, or more to taste
- 2 tbs butter
- 1 cup parmesan cheese
- 1/4 cup crème fraiche or natural yoghurt
- 1 tbs herb of your choice: basil, rosemary, sage

Method

1. Pour the water and salt into a heavy based pot and bring to the boil. Whisk in the polenta steadily and smoothly.
2. Turn the heat down and whisk vigorously until the mixture resembles whipped cream. Cover and simmer over low heat for 5–7 minutes. Turn the mixture once more with a wooden spoon before stirring in the herbs, cheese, yoghurt and butter.
3. Pour the mixture into a flat dish or baking tin and let it cool completely. This can be kept in the refrigerator for 2 days.
4. Cut the polenta into shapes of your choice. Brush a little oil on each piece. Place over a hot grill for a couple of minutes on each side until heated through and slightly charred if preferred.

HOMEMADE BREAD

Makes 1 Loaf

PREPARATION TIME: 15 MINUTES + PROVING TIME

COOKING TIME: 35 MINUTES

Ingredients

3 cups flour
1 packet instant yeast
1/2 tsp sugar
1 tsp salt
300 mL tepid water
2 tbs oil

For variety, add 100 gm of any of the following to the basic ingredients above:

Feta cheese and cooked spinach, making sure that all excess water has been squeezed out.

Sautéd onion rings with some fresh rosemary. Season with salt and pepper.

Sun-dried tomatoes, soaked in hot water to re-hydrate and chopped small.

Raisins soaked in masala or brandy and candied citrus peels.

Toasted walnuts with dried apricots.

Have fun and experiment with any other ingredients you can think of!

Method

1. Use enough oil to grease the bread tin. Dust a thin layer of flour over all the inner surfaces of the tin. Sift all dry ingredients into a mixing bowl. Make a well in the centre. Pour half of the water in the well and mix with a wide-based wooden spoon. Continue by adding the rest of the water little by little. Once the water has been added, start mixing the dough with your hands. Remember not to over mix. The secret to a good loaf of bread is "feather fingers".
2. Form the dough into a ball. Cover the mixing bowl with cling film or a damp tea towel and let the dough rise to double its original size. Knead the dough down again. Place it into the bread tin and let it rise to the edge of the tin. Brush the top with milk, then bake at 180°C in a pre-heated oven for 35 minutes. Once the 35 minutes are up, open the oven door gently, so as not to let too much cold air into the oven and insert a skewer into the bread loaf. If it comes out clean, then the bread is done. The other method is to knock on the crust of the bread. It is done when it sounds hollow. Turn the bread out to cool on a wire rack.

PANCAKES

Makes approximately 12–15 pancakes

PREPARATION TIME: 10 MINUTES

COOKING TIME: 5 MINUTES

Ingredients

1 cup self-raising flour
1 tbs salt (for savory)
or,
2 tbs sugar (for sweet)
1 cup milk
1 egg, beaten
1 tbs melted butter
Oil for frying

Method

1. Sift flour, salt or sugar (for savory or sweet base). Add milk and mix until smooth.
2. Finally add beaten egg and melted butter. Heat the pan and coat the surface with oil.
3. Pour enough batter to create a circle with a 10 cm diameter or your preferred size. As soon as the batter begins to bubble, flip over and cook until golden. Repeat until all the batter is finished.

Here are some interesting ingredients to add to the batter:

Simply select the desired ingredients listed below, add to the basic batter, mix thoroughly. Follow the cooking procedure as given above.

(Total weight of the ingredients should not exceed 150g per basic mix.)

- Bacon, onion or chives.
- Sweet corn kernels, chilli, coriander and lemon grass or lime zest.
- Zucchini, parmesan or pecorino cheese.
- Basil, tomatoes and rocket leaves.
- Spinach, feta and olives.
- Red or yellow peppers, olives, preserved lemons, or ground spices such as turmeric, ginger, cinnamon and paprika.
- Preserved ginger and citrus peels.
- Chocolate chips and candied fruits.

BREAD DISCS

Serves 4–6

PREPARATION TIME: 20 MINUTES + RESTING TIME

COOKING TIME: 5 MINUTES

Ingredients

2 cups white or whole wheat flour, a little more for dusting
2 tsp salt
1/2 tsp ground pepper
1 tbs sugar
1 egg, slightly beaten
1 cup boiling water
1 medium onion, halved and sliced
Oil

Method

1. Sift flour, salt and sugar into a large mixing bowl. Make a well in the centre. Add the boiling water little by little to form firm dough. Knead dough for a good minute or so. Wrap in cling film or put it back in the mixing bowl. Cover with a damp towel and let it rest for as long as possible.
2. Fry the onions in a little oil, season with salt and pepper. Let them sweat until softened. Set aside to cool.
3. Dust a board with more flour. Divide the dough into 6 portions. Roll each piece into a round disc with a diameter of 18–20cm. Divide the onions into 3 portions. Spread the first portion onto the first round and place another pastry round over to form a 'sandwich'. Seal the edges with egg mixture, press the edges down to secure. Roll lightly a few times. Repeat for the others. You should have 3 bread discs.
4. Heat the cooking surface over medium heat. When hot, oil the surface lightly. Place breads over the grill and turn over when little brown spots begin to show on the cooking side. Repeat this process once more on both sides until the breads are cooked. It should take between 2–3 minutes on each side.

SALSAS

CORN SALSA

Serves 4–6

Ingredients

4 medium-sized ears of corn on the cob
2–3 tomatoes, diced
1 cup coriander, chopped
1 cup spring onion, chopped
Juice of 1 lemon or lime
2 tbs fish sauce, or to taste
1 tsp sugar

Method

1. Boil the corn for 5–10 minutes. Once cooled, remove the kernels from the cobs.
2. Place all the ingredients in a bowl, mix well then serve.

My doctor told me to stop having
intimate dinners for four.
Unless there are three other people.

ORSON WELLES

GUACAMOLE SALSA

Serves 4–6

Ingredients

- 2 large or 4 small avocados (Hass would be first choice)
- 2–3 tomatoes (Roma or vine ripened ones are sweetest)
- 1 small or 1/2 large red onion
- Juice of 1 lime (you can include a little zest)
- Salt and pepper to taste
- 1/2 cup fresh coriander leaves, roughly chopped or hand torn

Method

1. Cut the avocados in half. Remove the pips with a swift snap of a knife.
2. Scoop the flesh out of its skin, chop it up and mash slightly.
3. Place the avocado flesh into a bowl. Add the chopped tomatoes, onion, lime juice and salt.
4. Mix well and serve with Tortilla chips or bread sticks.

PEPPERY RADISH SALSA

Serves 4–6

Ingredients

- 1 each red and yellow pepper, diced
- 1 bunch radish, thinly sliced (if the leaves are really fresh and tender, chop them up and add to the radish)
- 2–3 tomatoes, diced
- Juice of 1 lemon or lime
- 1 green chilli, minced
- Salt and pepper to taste
- 2 tbs vinegar
- 1 tsp honey
- 2 cloves garlic, minced (optional)
- 1 cup coriander, finely chopped

Method

1. Marinate the peppers and radish (not the leaves) in vinegar, honey and garlic for at least 30 minutes.
2. Combine all the ingredients, toss well and serve.

RUBS, MARINADES, GLAZES & SAUCES

CITRUS ANCHOVY RUB

Ingredients

Zest of 1 lime and lemon
1 clove garlic, minced
2 anchovy fillets, mashed
1/2 tsp coarsely ground salt

Method

1. Mix all ingredients well in a bowl, or use a pestle and mortar to form a finer paste.
2. This can be kept in the refrigerator for up to 3 weeks!
3. This is ideal for fish or poultry. Simply rub on meat before cooking.

GREEN RUB

Ingredients

2 tbs flat-leafed parsley
2 tbs mint
1 tsp lemon grass
2 tbs chives
2 tbs fennel tips, optional
2 tbs lemon pulp
2 tbs wholegrain mustard
1 tbs capers
2 cloves garlic
Peanuts or pine nuts, roasted and ground

Method

Chop all ingredients finely and mix well.

This is great for meat, fish or anything your heart desires.

Tomatoes and oregano make it Italian; wine and tarragon make it French. Sour cream makes it Russian; lemon and cinnamon make it Greek. Soy sauce makes it Chinese; garlic makes it good.

ALICE MAY BROCK

SUMAC RUB

Ingredients

1 tbs sumac
Citrus zests from 1 lemon and 1 orange dried or fresh
2 tbs parsley
1 tsp garlic
2 tsp salt

Method

Mix all ingredients well.

Suitable for fish and chicken.

WORLDLY RUB

Ingredients

1 tbs ground cumin
1 tbs paprika
1 tsp onion flakes
2 tbs dry rose petals
1 tbs salt
1 tbs tumeric
2 tbs chilli flakes
1 tbs tamarind paste
3 tbs fresh parsley, finely chopped
2 tbs pine nuts, toasted and ground
1/2 tsp pepper

Method

1. Combine all ingredients and mix well.
2. Store in an airtight jar in refrigerator.
3. Use the rub within 2 weeks.

5 FRAGRANT SPICES RUB

Ingredients

2 tsp fennel seeds
1 tsp ginger
2 tsp star anise
2 tsp cinnamon
1 tsp cloves
1 tsp sesame seeds
2 tsp salt
1 tsp garlic

Method

1. For the cheats: use ground spices. Simply toast all spices in a dry frying pan until the fragrance is released.
2. Remember to stir with a wooden spoon constantly.
3. Remove from heat before adding the salt flakes and minced garlic. Alternatively, you can dry fry all the barks and seeds until smoke begins to emerge.
4. Grind up all dry spices using a coffee bean mill or a pestle and mortar.
5. Add salty flakes, minced ginger and garlic.
6. Suitable for all meats.

BEER MARINADE

Ingredients

1 can of beer
1 lemon, roughly chopped
1 tbs coarse salt
2 tbs oil
1/2 tsp sugar

Method

1. Rub salt into the lemon pieces. For the best result, leave it overnight or longer.
2. When ready to marinade meat, combine all ingredients then pour over meat.
3. This goes extremely well with game and other tougher cuts of meats.

GARLIC OR GINGER VINAIGRETTE

Ingredients

2–4 cloves garlic or 10 cm root ginger, minced or grated
White or red wine vinegar
Sugar and salt to taste

Method

1. Mix all ingredients and use within 1 week, if refrigerated.
2. Best used for poached or steamed poultry or any seafood.
3. Use it to marinate a mixture of cooked seafood.
4. Also, serve on a bed of chilled salad leaves as a dressing.

POULTRY MARINADE

Ingredients

1 cup natural yoghurt
1 medium onion, finely grated
1 sprig rosemary, chopped
1 sprig thyme, chopped
1 bay leaf
Salt and pepper
1 tbs cayenne pepper or paprika can be added if you desire a spicier marinade

Method

1. Combine all ingredients and mix well.
2. Refrigerate and use within 3 days.

SECRET MARINADE

Ingredients

1 cup tomato sauce
1 cup molasses; 1/3 honey or 1/4 cup sugar
1/2 cup oil
2 or more cloves of crushed garlic
1 tbs salt
1/2 tbs black pepper, crushed
juice of 1/2 a lemon
1 bay leaf
1/2 tsp cloves or whole if preferred

Method

1. Mix all ingredients and store in bottle until needed.
2. This can last up to a month in the refrigerator.
3. Soy sauce, hoisin or plum sauce can be added for variation.

I cook with wine, sometimes I even add it to the food.

W C FIELDS

WINE MARINADE

Ingredients

1/2 cup red or white wine
1 tsp star anise
1 bay leaf
5 pepper corns
1 whole lemon, sliced
3 whole cloves garlic, flattened with blade of a knife
1 tsp sugar
Salt and pepper to taste

Method

1. Combine all ingredients.

   Feel free to add thyme, sage, rosemary or any herb of your choice.

YOGHURT MARINADE

Ingredients

1 cup natural yoghurt
2 tbs marsala
1 tbs black mustard seeds, ground
2 tbs toasted sesame seeds, ground
1/4 cup olive oil
Juice of 1/2 or 1 lemon
1 pinch of sugar
Salt and pepper to taste

Method

1. Combine all ingredients.
2. The marinade can be kept up to 1 week in the refrigerator.
3. It can be used on poultry, meat or fish.

All these glazes are great for basting meat, especially poultry and game. They will last for as long as jams if stored in the refrigerator.

APRICOT GLAZE

Ingredients

2 tbs apricot jam
1 tbs chopped apricot
2 tbs fruit chutney
1 tbs tomato puree
2 tbs Verjuice/ sherry /dessert wine
Juice of 1/4 lemon
Pinch of salt

Method

1. Combine all ingredients in a saucepan.
2. Bring to the boil over medium to low heat.
3. Simmer for a further minute or two, until all have integrated and the mixture is glistening.

What is patriotism but the love of the food one ate as a child?
LIN YUTANG

HONEY GLAZE

Ingredients

2 tbs treacle honey
4 tbs honey
1/2 tsp ground cloves
1/2 tsp ground all spice
1/2 tsp ground ginger or 1 tbs fresh root ginger
2 tbs orange juice
2 tsp English mustard powder
1 tbs brandy

Method

1. Stir all the ingredients together and bring them to boil.
2. Cool and store in the refrigerator until needed.

PINEAPPLE GLAZE

Ingredients

¼ pineapple, liquidised with a little juice or water
3 tbs brown sugar/treacle
1 tbs mustard powder
1 tsp mint, finely minced

Method

1. Combine the first three items and bring them to the boil.
2. Turn off the heat, add the mint and allow to cool.
3. Store in a sterilised jar until needed.

BARBECUE SAUCE

Ingredients

1 small onion, grated
2 garlic cloves, minced
5 tbs chutney
5 tbs tomato sauce
2 tbs oil
1 tbs English mustard powder, or
2 tbs Dijon mustard
2 tbs molasse or brown sugar
2 tbs brandy or sherry

Method

1. Bring all ingredients to the boil in a small saucepan.
2. Stir and allow to simmer until the sauce is syrupy and thickened.
3. Use within 2 weeks if refrigerated.

Cheese is milk's leap toward immortality.

CLIFF FADIMAN

SWEET SPICY TOMATO SAUCE

Ingredients

1 onion, finely chopped
2 cloves garlic, minced
1 tsp fresh ginger root, minced
5 tomatoes, finely chopped
1 tbs tomato puree
200 ml passata
1 tsp cinnamon
1 tsp cloves
2 tbs oil
1/2 cup water
6 dried apricots, diced
2 tbs brown sugar
1 tbs brandy/sherry
1–2 chillis, minced
3 tbs coriander, roughly chopped

Method

1. Dissolve the sugar over a gentle heat.
2. Add in brandy or sherry and apricot. Set aside.
3. Fry the onion, garlic and ginger until opaque, then stir in the tomatoes, puree/passata and the ground spices.
4. Bring to the boil, add water, chilli and coriander.
5. Bring it back to the boil, then turn heat down and simmer for a further 10 minutes.
6. Remove from heat and allow to cool.
7. Store in sterilised jars in the refrigerator for up to 2 weeks.

CHILLI SAUCE

Ingredients

6–10 chillis (depending on strength), green and red
2 cloves garlic, minced
1 tsp fresh ginger root, minced
1/2 cup tomato puree/passata
1 tsp salt
1 lemon juice, plus zest
1 cup sugar

Method

1. De-seed the chillis. Place all ingredients, except the sugar, in a blender and grind to a thick paste.
2. Place the sugar and the paste into a saucepan. Bring to the boil. Simmer until sauce is glistening.
3. It is similar to jam making, except the sauce should be a little thinner. Remove from heat and cool. Place in a sterilised jar or container. It is delicious with poultry, cheese and ice cream.
4. Store in the refrigerator for up to 4 weeks.

ARB
4X4 ACCESSORIES
ARB TOURING
ARB
TURBO DIESEL V6

Lemon & Garlic Chicken

Serves 4–6

PREPARATION TIME: 25 MINUTES + RESTING TIME

COOKING TIME: 60-90 MINUTES

There's nothing like a good spit over the campfire. The best part about this recipe is that you can prepare and marinate this at home before you leave and then freeze it. All the hard work is done before you even roll out the swag

Ingredients

2kg chicken thighs
¼ cup olive oil
2 tbsp lemon juice
2 tbsp dry thyme
2 tbsp dry oregano
5 cloves garlic, minced
Salt and pepper

To make the marinade: Whisk the olive oil, lemon juice, herbs and garlic in a bowl and season with salt and pepper to taste.

Method

1. Add your choice of marinade to the chicken thighs, ensuring the marinade is well mixed through and massaged into the meat. We usually like to do this in a large zip lock bag.
2. Let the chicken marinate for at least four hours, preferably overnight. Chicken can be frozen at this point for use at a later date.
3. Prepare your campfire so that it is mostly hot coals. Take the spit attachment and add on the first fork.
4. Skewer each chicken thigh through the middle, turning each piece by 45 degrees to try and ensure an even shape. Add the end fork and compress the chicken stack as tightly as possible to prevent the chicken spit from spinning on the spike. Reserve the leftover marinade for basting.

Frying Pan Lasagne

Serves 6 (hungry campers).

PREPARATION TIME: 5 MINUTES

COOKING TIME: 10 MINUTES

Life on the road is so much easier with a little effort before you leave. We always make up a huge batch of Bolognese sauce and freeze it. If you don't have time, you can always buy pre-made Bolognese sauce from the supermarket (but there is nothing like the home made stuff).

Ingredients

375g fresh lasagne sheets
60g baby spinach leaves
900g ready-made bolognese pasta sauce
1 ½ cups water
1 ½ cups firm ricotta
1 ½ cups grated pizza cheese
Fresh basil

Method

1. Tear each lasagne sheet lengthways into three long strips.
2. Using a large deep frying pan, add the spinach, pasta sauce and water. Stir to combine.
3. Insert the pasta strips into the sauce, standing upright on long sides. Sprinkle with the ricotta and pizza cheeses. Bring to the boil and simmer, covered for five minutes until pasta is tender. Remove from heat and let stand for five minutes.
4. Sprinkle with basil leaves and serve.

Peanut Butter Chicken

Serves 6–8 (hungry campers).

PREPARATION TIME: 10 MINUTES

COOKING TIME: 20 MINUTES

Ingredients

2 cups smooth peanut butter
1/3 cup soy sauce
½ tsp garlic powder
1/3 cup brown sugar
1 tsp red chilli flakes
2 tsp apple cider vinegar
¼ cup honey
1 tsp cracked black pepper
1 kg chicken thighs
olive oil

Method

1. Preheat a hotplate over a campfire or bbq, making sure it is kept at a very low heat.
2. Mix together all ingredients except the chicken thighs and olive oil, you should end up with a thick, sticky paste.
3. Pat the chicken thighs dry with paper towel.
4. Using your hands, smear the paste over the chicken thighs. It doesn't matter if they aren't evenly covered, just try to get all the paste over the chicken.
5. Ensuring the hotplate is not too hot, add enough olive oil to cover the plate and then add the chicken thighs. Because of the honey and sugar in the recipe, the sauce can easily burn so make sure you keep the heat low. Cook the thighs for around 10 minutes and then turn (try not to turn more than once as you will lose all the crispy, peanutty goodness on the outside).
6. Once the chicken thighs are cooked through, transfer to a plate. Give the remaining peanut sauce on the hotplate a good stir and spoon over the chicken. Serve with mac & cheese or baked potatoes.

Campfire BBQ Ribs & Chilli Cheese Fries

Serves 4 (hungry campers).

PREPARATION TIME: 10 MINUTES + RESTING TIME

COOKING TIME: 120-180 MINUTES

Ingredients

3 racks ribs
1 sachet dry meat rub
1 red onion
1 red capsicum
1 yellow capsicum
1 bottle BBQ sauce (we used Sweet Baby Rays) 1 bottle stout
Camp oven

Chilli Cheese Fries ingredients

1 bag frozen French fries
2 cans beef chilli
3 handfuls pizza cheese
1 tin foil tray
Aluminium foil to cover

Method

1. Begin by rubbing the dry meat rub over both sides of your rib racks.
2. Slice the onion and capsicum and put into the base of the camp oven. Top with the ribs and pour the entire bottle of BBQ sauce on top. Repeat with the entire bottle of stout, cover and cook in the campfire for approximately 2-3 hours (trying to achieve a constant temperature of around 180 degrees Celsius). Check the ribs regularly to ensure the sugar in the recipe does not burn.
3. Take your tin foil tray and add the entire bag of French fries. (Optional: cover with foil and cook in campfire for around 20 minutes if you like your chilli cheese fries crispy). Pour over both cans of chilli beef and top with three handfuls of pizza cheese. Cover with foil and cook on the campfire for around 30 minutes or until cheese is brown and bubbly.

Orange Chocolate Cakes

Serves 6 (hungry campers).

PREPARATION TIME: 20 MINUTES

COOKING TIME: 30 MINUTES

Ingredients

1 packet of chocolate cake mix
eggs, milk & butter (amounts as per cake mix) 6 oranges
aluminium foil
or
1 camp oven with trivet

Method

1. Prepare the chocolate cake mix as per packet instructions.
2. Slice the top off each orange and scoop out the pulp. Fill each orange with chocolate cake mix and replace the top or lid of the orange.
3. Wrap each orange in two layers of foil and place in the coals of a campfire.

or

Place each orange on a trivet in a camp oven and place the camp oven on the coals of your campfire.

Cook for 30 minutes or until cake is cooked through.

Cookies and Cream Cheesecake

Serves 4-8 campers (depending on serving size).

PREPARATION TIME: 15 MINUTES

COOKING TIME: 120 MINUTES

Ingredients

4 tbsp butter, melted
1 packet choc ripple biscuits
2 blocks cream cheese (room temperature) ¾ cup condensed milk
Pack of Oreo biscuits

Method

1. Place the choc ripple biscuits into a large zip lock bag or clean tea towel and crush to a crumb. Mix in the melted butter.
2. Place the cream cheese and condensed milk in a bowl and whisk until smooth (does take a little elbow grease).
3. Place the choc biscuit crumb into a jar, mug or bowl and press down to compress to a one-centimetre thick base. The size of your receptacle will determine how many cheesecakes you end up with but we found we made eight small ¾-cup jar cheesecakes from this recipe.
4. Portion out your cheesecake mixture between your jars and top with crumbled Oreo biscuits.
5. Place in fridge for two hours, then serve.

The Amazing Portable Dream-Pot®

This simple to use non-electrical indoor and outdoor multifunctional Dream-Pot® can be used as a:
• thermo cooker • rice cooker • yoghurt maker • cooler • bain-marie — one Dream-Pot® does it all!

At home or when travelling, the Dream-Pot® is the perfect partner for indoor and outdoor use, cooking delicious and nutritious 1 or 2 course meals together. The Dream-Pot® is simple to use and very easy to clean.

The Dream-Pot® is an attractive appliance containing one or two inner pots with an ergonomically designed carry handle. The outer shell contains special heat insulating material. The stainless steel inner pots (which are your 'saucepans') can be used on either electric or gas stoves to start the cooking process.

Once the inner pots are placed into the Dream-Pot®, it is used to thermo-cook or to maintain hot or cold temperatures without the need for constant fuel or power. The food cannot boil over, burn or dry out in the Dream-Pot® and requires no further attention or supervision while your meal is cooking. This allows the convenience of completing other tasks without the need for constant monitoring.

The features of easy operation, non-electrical convenience, safety, stability and cost savings on time and energy (such as gas or electricity) makes the Dream-Pot® an indispensible and versatile appliance.

HOW TO USE YOUR DREAM-POT®

THERMO COOKS

Safe and simple to use.
Simply place ingredients into the inner pot and bring to the boil and cover with the lid. Gently boil on your stove for the required time as per your recipe. Then place the inner pot directly into the Dream-Pot®, close the lid of the insulated pot. Thermo cooking will start. The food completes cooking in its own heat.
After the necessary minimum thermo cooking time, the delicious food is ready to eat.

Stainless steel lid

Small 2 litre stainless steel inner pot for 5 and 6 litre models.

Large stainless steel inner pot for 5 and 6 litre models.

Dream-Pot®

EASY COOKING PROCESS

Put ingredients into inner pot. Place on stove. Bring to boil, then continue to boil for short required time, with the lid on (as stated in each recipe.)

Transfer inner pot into the Dream-Pot® and close the lid

Let stand to cook using its own heat for the minimum stated time. No constant stirring or checking is required.

After required cooking time in Dream-Pot®, serve either immediately or when required up to 8 hours later (as per safety instructions on facing page).

3 LITRE DREAM-POT®

- The 3 litre Dream-Pot® maximum heat retention time is between 5 to 6 hours, when the inner pot is 80% full. Heat retention time mentioned in this book applies to the larger 5 and 6 litre Dream-Pots®.
- Most recipes may be used in all sizes of the Dream-Pot®. Quantities used may need to be changed when using the 3 litre model. Certain recipes cannot be used due to the 3 litre model containing one inner pot only.
- Disregard references to using the small and large inner pots together (mentioned in some recipes) as this applies to larger 5 and 6 litre Dream-Pots® only.

CARE AND CLEANING

DREAM-POT®	To clean the Dream-Pot®, wipe over with a soft cloth which has been rinsed in warm soapy water. Do not immerse the Dream-Pot® in water or any other liquids. Dry thoroughly with a soft cloth.
INNER POT LID	The lid is immersible in water for cleaning. Dry thoroughly with a soft cloth. Dishwasher safe.
INNER POT	The inner pot can be immersed into water and cleaned with detergent. Dry thoroughly with a soft cloth. Dishwasher safe.

BASIC SAFETY PRECAUTIONS

When using the Dream-Pot®, basic precautions should be followed.

- When using large inner pot on the stove, keep the handle upright.
- Do not heat the insulated Dream-Pot® on a gas or electric stove, oven or flame.
- Do not heat an empty inner pot.
- Do not put any food or beverage into the insulated Dream-Pot®—always use the inner pots.
- Do not use harsh abrasives, caustic cleaners or oven cleaners when cleaning the Dream-Pot®.
- Do not use the Dream-Pot® for other than its intended use.
- IMPORTANT: Always observe normal food hygiene practices.
- Only heat with medium heat. Do not heat with high heat.
- It is safe to leave your cooked food in the Dream-Pot® for up to 8 hours, depending on quantity.

  If you need your meal to be in safe temperature zone for at least this time, you must ensure the pot is 80% full. This could be one large meal using the large inner pot only: two courses cooked together using large inner pot and the small inner pot at the one time: or one smaller meal using the small inner pot (sitting over 2 litres of boiling water in the large inner pot to fill up the gap.)

  The more volume of food in the Dream-Pot® the longer the heat retention.

CHICKEN, SWEET CORN & VEGETABLE SOUP

Ingedients

- 1 swede
- 1 turnip
- 3 sticks celery
- 1 large potato
- 1 tbs paprika
- 1 large onion
- 1 zucchini
- 1 large carrot
- 1 parsnip
- 250 gm frozen mixed vegetables
- 1 1/2 litres boiling water
- 1 pkt. cream of chicken soup
- 1 pkt. chicken noodle soup
- 1 cup cold water
- 1 1/2 tsp. garlic powder
- 1/2 tsp. pepper, salt to taste
- 1 can sweet corn incl. juice
- 1 1/2 chicken breast fillets

Method

1. Cut up the vegetables into chunky pieces and whiz in a food processor or dice into small cubes. Dice the potato.
2. Place these vegetables into large inner pot. Add the frozen vegetables. Pour over the boiling water. Bring to the boil, stirring intermittently.
3. Add the soup mixes (thoroughly mixed into the cold water), garlic powder, salt, pepper, sweet corn and diced chicken breast. Stir well to combine.
4. Return to the boil, reduce heat and gently boil for 10 minutes with lid on, stirring intermittently.
5. Transfer into the Dream-Pot for minimum cooking time.

HINTS

For simple change of flavours, use diced gravy beef and 2 packets of Hearty Beef Soup. Add any type of vegetable (pumpkin, broccoli, cauliflower, etc). As vegetarian alternative, use 2 packets of Spring Vegetable Soup. A can of tomatoes also adds another flavour.

Any left over soup from your meal can be stored directly in the stainless steel inner pot in the fridge. Serve with hot crusty bread. YUM!

RICOTTA & SPINACH LASAGNA

Ingredients

1 box San Remo gluten free lasagna sheets
250 gm chopped spinach (fresh or frozen) or fresh baby spinach 3/4 packet of pre-pack
250 gm ricotta cheese
2 egg yolks
400 gm tin of crushed tomatoes with basil
salt, pepper and garlic powder
5 cheese slices

Method

1. Thaw the frozen spinach and squeeze out excess moisture between layers of paper towels.
2. Mix together the cheese, spinach, egg yolk and seasonings.
3. Assemble the lasagna. Lightly spray the inside of the large loaf pan. Cover the base with some crushed tomatoes.
4. Layer a lasagna sheet over the tomato. Snap the corners to fit flat, then fill any gaps with pieces of trimmed lasagna to completely cover the tomato.
5. Spoon over a layer of cheese mixture.
6. Repeat the layers, ending with the cheese mixture.
7. Place cheese slices on top, overlapping and trimming to cover the entire top of the assembled lasagna.
8. Cover the loaf pan with buttered or sprayed foil.
9. Place a trivet (use 5 empty sandwich tuna cans) in the large inner pot.
10. Place the assembled lasagna onto the trivets and pour hot water to come half way up the side of the loaf pan.
11. Bring to the boil and maintain a gentle boil for 20 minutes. Check occasionally to ensure that the water is continually gently boiling.
12. Transfer to the Dream-Pot® for the minimum cooking time.

SOY CHICKEN

Ingredients

- 1 fresh chicken (if frozen thaw well) wash and dry well
- 1 bunch shallots, chopped
- 3 cups soy sauce low salt
- 2 tsp ground cumin

Hot water to cover

Method

1. Place chicken into larger inner pot.
2. Add remaining ingredients. Ensure chicken is totally covered with liquid.
3. Cover and bring to boil, stirring occasionally.
4. Gently boil for 15 minutes.
5. Without lifting the lid, transfer to Dream-Pot® for at least 1 hour minimum.

NOTE:

Thermo cooking time may vary according to size of the chicken.

Soy sauce quantity may be adjusted to own taste.

Size 20 chicken or smaller may be cooked in the 5 litre or 6 litre model.

VEAL & BACON LOAF

Ingredients

- 500 gm minced veal
- 250 gm lean bacon (minced or chopped finely)
- 1 cup breadcrumbs
- 2 eggs lightly beaten
- 2 hard boiled eggs optional
- 1 tbp chopped parsley
- 1/2 cup chopped celery
- Salt and pepper to taste

Method

1. Mix all ingredients together.
2. Spray two 665 gm soup tins well with a cooking spray.
3. Divide the mixture evenly between the tins. Cover each tin securely with greased foil.
4. Place the tins in the base of the large inner pot and pour boiling water around the tins until water comes approximately half to two-thirds up the sides of the tins.
5. Bring to the boil, covered with lid. Adjust heat and maintain a slow boil for 15 minutes, checking intermittently.
6. Transfer into the Dream-Pot® for 2 hours minimum.

OPTIONAL:

Place hard boiled eggs upright into the centre of the tins and pack meat mixture under and around the eggs.

CORNED SILVERSIDE

Ingredients

1 1/2 kg piece corned silverside
1 cup brown sugar
1 cup brown vinegar
1 tablespoon french mustard
Hot water

Method

1. Place all ingredients into large inner pot. Cover until at least 2/3 full with hot water and bring to the boil stirring occasionally. Cover with stainless steel lid.
2. Gently boil on low heat for 20 minutes, stirring occasionally.
3. Transfer to the Dream-Pot® for 3 hours minimum.

NOTE:

To cook potatoes, carrots and onions with the corned silverside—scrub the vegetables, leave whole, do not peel the onion. Add to the corned meat in the last 10 minutes of the boiling time on the stove. For example, maintain the corned silverside on a gentle boil for 10 minutes, add the vegetables, bring back to the boil and then time for a second 10 minutes, gently boiling.

Pickled pork may be substituted for the corned silverside.

LAMB IRISH STEW

Ingredients

6–8 lamb forequarter chops, trimmed
1 large onion
300 gm frozen mixed vegetables
2 potatoes cut into large cubes
1 pkt. cream of chicken soup
1 pkt. chicken noodle soup
Salt and pepper
1 tsp garlic powder (optional)

Method

1. Place chopped onion, lamb chops, mixed vegetables and potatoes into large inner pot. Cover with freshly boiling water.
2. Bring to the boil, gently stirring occasionally. Mix together the soup with 1 cup of cold water and add stirring into the stew mixture.
3. Add salt, pepper and garlic powder to taste and bring to the boil.
4. Reduce heat and boil gently for 10 minutes with the lid on. Stir occasionally.
5. Without lifting lid, transfer into the Dream-Pot® for minimum cooking time.

HINT:

Stir in half a cup of finely chopped parsley prior to serving.

LAMB HOT POT ROAST

Ingredients

- 1/2 leg of lamb (bone in – 1.4 kg average) trim off the fat
- Virgin olive oil
- 1/2 cup (approximately) teriyaki marinade (original flavour)
- Plain flour
- 1 large oven bag

Method

1. Open up the oven bag and sit in the large inner pot.
2. Heat oil in a large non-stick frying pan.
3. Roll the lamb in the flour and brown all over in the pan.
4. Pour the teriyaki marinade intermittently over the lamb to colour. Turn until brown and crisp (2–3 minutes).
5. Place the browned lamb into the oven bag, place 3 tablespoons flour around the meat.
6. Remove the oven bag on to the table and with your hands squeeze the air out of the bag and tie into a knot close to the meat. Also tie around the knot with the strip off the top of the oven bag to make the bag watertight. Place into the large inner pot.
7. Carefully pour hot water into the inner pot (not directly over the bag) until the water covers the bag, to come to approximately 2–3 cm from the top of the pot.
8. Bring to the boil, cover with lid, lower and adjust the heat to maintain a gentle boil for 30 minutes. It is important to check intermittently that a gentle boil is maintained.
9. Tranfer to the Dream-Pot® for the required minimum cooking time.
10. Prior to serving, carefully remove the bag and place onto a suitable dish. Snip one corner of the bottom of the bag to allow the gravy to flow out into the dish. Remove the lamb and add to the gravy.

NOTE:

Check that the bone is smooth to prevent the bag from splitting. If any larger than half a leg is used, have the butcher bone it out and roll. If wishing to cook potatoes and carrots with the lamb, after completing Step 4, cut into smaller pieces and toss the vegetables in the flour, sear in the pan and add to the bag with the lamb, prior to sealing the bag.
Commence the cooking in the morning and serve for the midday meal or commence at lunchtime for the evening meal.

POACHED PEARS
IN GRAPE JUICE

Ingredients

4 whole small pears-peeled leaving the stem intact
2 1/2 cups dark grape juice
Juice of an orange
1/4 tsp cinnamon
6 cloves
2 tbs cornflour

Method

1. Mix the grape juice, orange juice and spices together in the small inner pot, and bring gently to the boil.
2. Thicken with the cornflour mixed with a little water and poured into the juices.
3. Stir continually and gently boil for a few minutes.
4. Place the pears into the boiling juice and spoon the juice over the fruit.
5. Continue to boil gently, covered for 5 minutes.
6. Place into the large inner pot (over 2 litres of boiling water) which is sitting in the Dream-Pot®.
7. Cover with the stainless steel lid and close the lid of the Dream-Pot®.

NOTE:

Instead of grape juice, substitute water only with pink food colouring.

APPLE CRUMBLE

Ingredients

400 gm tin pie apples
3 tbs SR flour
3 tbs brown sugar
2 tsp shredded coconut
1 heaped dsp butter
Nutmeg

Method

1. Place the pie apples, divided equally, into 2 small pie dishes.
2. Rub butter into flour with fingertips until the mixture is fine. Mix in the sugar and coconut.
3. Spoon the mixture equally onto the pie apples, and press the mixture down with the back of the spoon.
4. Sprinkle with nutmeg generously.
5. Cover each pie dish securely with buttered or sprayed alfoil, and tuck in around the rim.
6. Place each dish into the inner pots (large and small). Pour hot water around the pie dishes until the water comes approximately halfway up the side of the pie dishes.
7. Cover each with a stainless steel lid and bring to the boil, checking occasionally that the water is continually boiling for 5 minutes.
8. Transfer the large inner pot into the Dream-Pot®, then place the smaller inner pot into the large inner pot. Cover with the stainless steel lid. Close the Dream-Pot® and leave the apple crumbles cook together for the minimum required cooking time. (They are both cooking together at the same time.)
9. Once removed from the Dream-Pot®, allow the apple crumbles to stand (uncovered of the foil) for 10 minutes to enable the top crust to firm.
10. Serve with custard.

TOMATO & OLIVE DAMPER

Ingredients

1 1/2 cups SR flour
150 mL tomato soup
1 tsp mixed herbs
1/2 tsp garlic powder
1 dsp olive oil
1/4 cup sliced olives
1/4 cup diced capsicum
Ground sea salt
Pinch baking powder
Pinch salt
1/4 cup water

Method

1. Put 2 litres boiling water into large inner pot. Place small inner pot, sprayed with cooking spray, over the boiling water. Cover with lid and boil on the stove as a double saucepan, to preheat while the damper is being mixed. You will note that the steam will be visible between the two inner pots. Keep it boiling well!
2. Sift SR flour into a bowl.
3. Add soup, herbs, garlic, salt and water. Mix with a knife to a soft dough.
4. Place onto a floured board and knead gently.
5. Pat out to a round approximately 17 cm across.
6. Brush lightly with olive oil. Scatter olives, capsicum and ground sea salt over the top.
7. Remove the lid from the small inner pot and carefully tranfer the round of dough into the inner pot, using an egg lifter.
8. Replace the lid and continue to double boil for 20 minutes. Don't lift the lid.
9. Quickly transfer into the Dream-Pot® for a further 30 minutes.
10. Tip damper out onto a teatowel. Serve warm with cheese, ham or salad vegetables.

SCONES

Ingredients

- 1 1/2 cups SR flour
- 1/2 tsp baking powder
- 1 dsp sugar
- 1 dsp soft butter
- 1 egg
- 1/4 tsp salt
- 1/4 cup water
- 1/4 cup milk

Method

1. Put 2 litres boiling water into large inner pot. Place small inner pot, sprayed well with cooking spray, over the boiling water. Cover with lid and boil on the stove as a double saucepan, to preheat while the scones are being mixed. You will note that the steam will be visible between the two inner pots. Keep it boiling well!
2. Mix together the flour, baking powder, sugar and salt with a fork.
3. Rub in butter with fingertips.
4. Mix together water, egg and milk and add to flour mixture.
5. Combine with a fork to make a moist dough.
6. Spoon onto a floured surface.
7. Press out into a round with floured hands approximately 17 cm across.
8. Cut into 12 rounds with a 5 cm scone cutter and place into small inner pot.
9. Replace lid and continue to double boil on the stove for 15 minutes. Do not lift the lid.
10. Transfer double pots quickly into Dream-Pot for a further 15 minutes minimum.
11. Tip scones out onto a tea towel. Serve with jam and cream.

NOTE:

If using 3 cups SR flour adjust liquid to make a moist dough. By doubling the ingredients the 12 scones will turn out higher. Adjust liquid quantity to make a moist soft dough if necessary—may need a little less than double. Currants may be added to flour.

Thermos Shuttle Chef

CARE INSTRUCTIONS

Wash and rinse the inner cooking pot and lid thoroughly before first use and after each use. The inner cooking pot and lid may be washed in dishwater.

The outer insulated container should be wiped clean with a soft cloth and mild detergent. The lid may be removed easily from the transport container by lifting the lid slightly and pulling forward to release the hinge. Do not immerse the transport container to avoid water becoming trapped in the base.

Do not use abrasive cleansers or scubbers as they may dull the finish.

Do not use bleach or cleaners containing chlorine on any parts of the product.

INSTRUCTIONS FOR USE

1. Remove the inner cooking pot from the outer insulated container.
2. Assemble ingredients and seasonings in the inner cooking pot.
3. Place the lid on the inner cooking pot and place on stove. Keep the handle in the upright position to keep it from becoming too hot.
4. Heat the inner cooking pot to a boil over medium heat. Boil for several minutes according to recipe requirements. High heat is not recommended.

5. Remove the covered inner cooking pot from the heat source and place it into the outer insulated container. Close the insulated container lid and rotate the handle forward to secure the lid.
6. The contents of the pot will stay hot and continue to cook after the inner cooking pot is placed inside the outer container. Serve when desired or after the cooking time as designated by the recipe.

CAUTIONS

- Do not microwave.
- Do not place the outer insulated container (outer pot) directly on a heat source. Direct heat will damage the container and the plastic parts will melt or burn.
- Keep out of reach of children when product contains hot liquids or food.
- System must be kept upright during transport.
- Do not overfill product. Hot liquids or food can scald user.
- Dairy or other liquids that spoil easily should not be kept in product for prolonged periods.
- Do not sctrach the insulated transport container with sharp utensils or the vacuum insulating structure may be damaged.
- Do not take apart or modify the product.
- It is normal that the outer insulated container and its lid become warm once the heated inner cooking pot is placed inside. However, if the inner cooking pot has been heated too long, the temperature inside the container may be too high. After putting the inner cooking pot into the outer container, you may feel the exterior of the outer container become slightly hot. Set the transport container aside for a few minutes and it will cool down and reach the proper temperature.
- Do not heat the inner cooking pot when it is empty.
- Calcium or salts can leave stains or pitting on the inner cooking pot surface. This is normal and is not considered a manufacturing defect. Slight pitting is harmless and will not affect the performance.
- Avoid sudden changes of temperature. Do not immerse the pot in cold water while hot.

FOOD SAFETY INFORMATION

- Most cases of food borne illness are due to unsafe cooking, holding and reheating temperatures. Unsafe temperatures allow harmful bacteria that might be present in food to grow. To prevent bacterial growth, maintian food at safe temperatures; 5 degrees C or colder, or 60 degrees C or hotter.
- The Thermos Shuttle Cook & Carry System can safely maintain many foods at 60 degrees C or hotter for eight hours or more.
- Food must be handled safely before placing it in the insulated transport container.

THE FOLLOWING GUIDELINES WILL HELP YOU TO MAXIMISE THE PRODUCT PERFORMANCE FOR MAXIMUM FOOD SAFETY.

- Always cook or reheat food in the Shuttle Chef inner cooking pot — do not transfer heated foods into the inner cooking pot.
- Place the inner cooking pot into the outer insulated container only after the contents have been brought to a boil.

- Liquid foods such as soup or spaghetti sauce can safely maintain hot temperatures longer than solid foods, such as macaroni and cheese, and rice. Solid foods should not be held in the Shuttle Chef for more than 4 hours. It is the nature of these types of food to lose heat more quickly.

YOU CAN SAFELY KEEP LIQUID FOOD HOT FOR UP TO EIGHT HOURS OR MORE.

- The amount of food placed into the Shuttle Chef inner cooking pot will affect how long the food can be safely kept hot. To maximise the time it can safely keep foods hot, fill the inner cooking pot to about 2.5 cm from the top. Both 3 litre pots must be used in the RPC6000 to maintain maximum temperature. If only using one pot, have boiling water in the second. The less food that is in the inner cooking pot the shorter time it can safely be kept hot.
- Rotate the handle on the pouter insulated container forward to an upright or forward position to secure the lid. This helps to ensure that heat is trapped inside the container as required to maintain proper temperatures.
- Do not open the lid of the insulated container or cooking pot until you are ready to eat the food. Each time the lid is opened, heat escapes, thus reducing the length of time food can be maintained at a safe temperature.
- Promptly refrigerate uneaten food.
- If food has been left in the Shuttle Chef Cook & Carry System for over two hours and is tepid when you open the pot, discard the food. Food can spoil rapidly when left at 60 degrees C and below.

PUMPKIN SOUP

Serves 6

Ingedients

40 gm of Butter
2 tbs of Olive Oil.
2 diced Onions.
3 cloves of Garlic.
3 rashers of Bacon trimmed and diced.
1 Massel Vegetable Stock cube.
1 kg Pumpkin (preferably Jap) peeled and cut into fairly large chunks.
6 stalks of Parsley.
1/2 a cup of Milk or Coconut Milk Powder.
Salt and Pepper to taste.
Sour Cream and chopped Chives for a garnish when serving.

Method

1. Gently fry the onions, garlic and bacon in the butter and olive oil in the pot over a medium heat.
2. Turn the heat down and add the pumpkin and enough boiling water to fill the pot to approximately 80% then add the stock cube, parsley, salt and pepper.
3. Bring the pot back to the boil and then simmer on a low heat for 5 minutes with the lid on.
4. Turn off the heat and transfer the pot to the outer Thermal Cooker and close the lid.
5. After at least 1 hour remove the inner pot and puree the soup with milk or coconut milk powder.
6. Serve and garnish with the sour cream and chopped chives.

SEAFOOD PAELLA

A delightful rich meal that is usually time consuming to cook but with the Shuttle Chef it is so simple and rewarding.

Ingredients

- 1/2 a tsp of saffron threads
- 3/4 cup of hot fish stock or chicken stock
- 1/4 of a cup of olive oil
- 1 large brown onion finely chopped
- 2 cloves of garlic crushed
- 2 medium ripe tomatoes chopped
- 1 cup of arborio rice
- 1 tsp of smoked paprika
- Salt and pepper to taste
- 1/2 a cup of frozen or dried peas
- 500 gm of marinara mix
- 8 small black mussels in their shells, scrubbed and debearded

Method

1. Stir the saffron threads in 2 tablespoons of boiling water.
2. Leave this to soak for 10 minutes.
3. Heat the oil in the inner saucepan and saute the onions over a low-medium heat until soft.
4. Add the garlic and tomatoes and cook over a medium heat until the tomatoes are thick and pulpy.
5. Add the rice and stir to coat with the mixture.
6. Stir in the hot stock, peas, paprika, salt and pepper and bring the mixture to a simmer.
7. Gently stir in the marinara mix.
8. Push the mussels into the mixture and close the lid.
9. Simmer for 1 minute.
10. Turn off the heat and transfer the saucepan into the vacuum insulated outer container.
11. Close the lid and leave for a minimum of 3/4 of an hour.
12. Discard any mussels that failed to open and serve.

SHUTTLE CHEF QUICHE

Ingredients

PASTRY

- 1 pkt suet mix
- 1/4 cup SR flour
- 1/3 cup cold water

FILLING

- 1 large or 2 small onions diced
- 4 rashers bacon diced
- 4 shallots finely sliced
- 1 tbs oil
- 1 cup baby spinach roughly chopped
- 2 tbs chopped parsley
- 1/2 cup grated tasty cheese
- 3 eggs
- 1/2 cup milk
- Slices tomato

Method

1. Make up suet pastry according to packet directions and place in fridge to chill.
2. Sauté onion and bacon in oil in Shuttle Chef inner saucepan.
3. Turn off heat and stir through baby spinach.
4. Add mix to shallots, parsley & cheese.
5. Whisk eggs and milk and pour over mix.
6. Grease and line with baking paper either in bain-marie or pudding tin.
7. Roll out pastry to fit the tin you are using.
8. Line with pastry, trimming evenly around the edge.
9. Pour mixture into pastry shell and cover with lid.
10. Place into Shuttle Chef inner saucepan with enough boiling water to come half way up the side of tin.
11. Simmer 30 minutes.
12. Transfer to outer for 2 hours or more.
14. Can be served hot or cold.

ROAST TURKEY AND CRANBERRY SAUCE

Ingedients

1–1.5 kg Boneless turkey leg roast
3 medium potatoes cut into halves
2 medium carrots, peeled and chunked
1 large onion diced
1 small sweet potato, peeled and chunked
1 packet of dried beans
275 gm jar of cranberry sauce
Water as required
Salt and Pepper to taste

Method

1. Place the turkey leg roast into the bottom of a 3 litre inner saucepan.
2. Fill in beside the roast with the diced onions and dried beans.
3. Empty the contents of the cranberry sauce over the roast and enough water to cover the ingredients.
4. Bring this to the boil and simmer with the lid on for a minimum of 20 minutes.
5. In the other 3 litre inner saucepan, place the chunky vegetables and cover with water.
6. Bring this to the boil and simmer with the lid on for 8 to 10 minutes.
7. *NOTE:* If using the 4.5 litre inner saucepan, just place the chunky vegetables in with the roast and cover with water.
8. Place the inner saucepans into the outer container and close the lid.
9. To serve, remove the roast and the vegetables and vigorously boil the remaining liquid until it is reduced by a half.
10. Pour this gravy over the individual servings.

MASSAMAN DUCK CURRY

A massaman curry is one of the most delicious dishes. It is thought to have arrived in Siam with the first Persian envoy to the court of Ayuthyia in the sixteenth century. Mr D has adapted this recipe for the Shuttle Chef from one published in Fresh Magazine and they have kindly given their permission for us to use it. This unusual version of Thai massaman curry is highly seasoned with tamarind and will delight you and your guests.

MASSAMAN DUCK CURRY

Ingredients

large duck breasts
2 star anise
2″ piece of cinnamon stick
3 bay leaves
6 cardamom pods
1 large onion chopped
3 tbs Mussaman paste
400 mL coconut milk
200 mL water & 1 chicken stock cube
small jar 100 gm of tamarind paste
1 tbs fish sauce
75 gm salted peanuts
350 gm potatoes cut into 2.5 cm cubes
small bunch of coriander leaves

Method

1. Put a frying pan on a high heat and when hot add the two duck breasts skin side down. Cook for 5–6 minutes until the skin is golden brown.
2. Turn the breasts over and cook for a further minute.
3. Remove from the pan slice the duck breasts and put to one side for later.
4. Heat 2 tbs of oil in the shuttle chef inner pot over a medium heat.
5. Add the star anise, cinnamon, bay leaves and cardamom and cook for 30 secs.
6. Add the chopped onion and cook for 4–6 minutes until golden.
8. Stir in the Massaman paste and cook for 1 minute.
9. Add the sliced duck and make sure that it is well coated with the mixture. Cook for 2 minutes.
10. Add the coconut milk, tamarind and fish sauce.
11. Add the chopped potatoes and make sure that they are nicely covered with the sauce. Bring to the boil.
12. Add 3/4 of the peanuts (saving the rest for garnish).
13. Turn the heat down to a simmer and cook for 5 minutes.
14. Put the lid on the inner pot and place it into the insulated outer pot.
15. Put the lid down and leave it to cook for 2 hours.
16. Serve with Jasmine rice and garnish with the remaining peanuts and the coriander.

CHINESE CURRIED CHICKEN

Because of China's vast size and age old culinary heritage it boasts a cuisine unmatched in its breadth and scope. Each small region of China has its own specialty dishes based on deep rooted traditions and availability of ingredients.

Cantonese food, cuisine of southern China has been long known and enjoyed in the West. Chefs draw upon the widest range of ingredients from all over China and her neighbours yet the food still remains distinctly Cantonese. You can even find curries that have been transformed into Cantonese dishes using a modest touch of curry spices, making them unrecognisable to anyone from India.

Ingredients

- 1 kg chicken thighs, de-boned and cut into bite sized pieces
- 2 tbs chinese wine or sherry
- 2 tbs corn flour
- 2 tbs of light soy sauce
- 1 tbs ghee (clarified butter) or vegetable oil
- 2 large onions, finely chopped
- 2 tbs ginger, grated
- 1 garlic clove, crushed and ground into a paste
- 1 tbs ground coriander
- 1 tsp turmeric
- 1/2 tsp chilli powder
- 1 tbs Madras curry powder
- 400 mL coconut milk
- 300 mL water
- 450g small potatoes, washed and unpeeled
- 1 lemongrass stem, tough outer leaves removed and then cut into thin slices
- 2 tsp shrimp paste
- 1 tbs sugar

Method

1. Marinade the chicken pieces in the Chinese wine, cornflour and soy sauce. Leave in the fridge for a minimum of 1 hour.
2. Heat the oil or ghee in the inner pot over a medium heat. Add the onion and stir-fry for 3 minutes, or until starting to soften but not let them brown.
3. Add the garlic and ginger and continue stir-frying for 30 seconds.
4. Reduce the heat to very low and leave to cook, stirring occasionally, until the onion is softened but not brown.
5. Stir in the coriander, turmeric, cumin, chilli and curry powder. Continue cooking over a very low heat for a further 5 minutes.
6. Add the chicken and marinade. Turn up the heat to medium and stir to coat it with the contents of the inner pot.
7. Add the coconut milk, water, potatoes, lemongrass and shrimp paste. Mix well and bring to the boil.
8. Reduce the heat and simmer for 10 minutes with the lid on.
9. Turn off the heat and place the inner pot into the insulated outer container.

11. Leave to thermal cook without heat for a minimum of 1 hour.
12. Serve with boiled rice.

CHICKEN CARBONARA

There is no need to precook the pasta in this dish.

STOVE TOP TIME: 4 MINUTES

SHUTTLE CHEF TIME: 60 MINUTES MINIMUM

Ingredients

MEATBALLS

400 gm of chicken mince
2 cloves of garlic
1 egg
1 tbs of finely chopped parsley
1 tbs of flour
A pinch of salt and pepper

SAUCE

2 tbs of oil
2 onions coarsely chopped
1 stick of celery sliced
2 zucchini's sliced
1 x 500 mL jar of carbonara sauce
500 mL of chicken stock
1/2 a cup of fresh parsley chopped
Salt and pepper to taste
1 1/2 cups of spiral pasta
Grated cheese to serve.

Method

1. Mix together the chicken mince, garlic, egg, finely chopped parsley, flour, salt and pepper.
2. Seperate into small portions.
3. Roll these portions into balls approximately 2 cm in diameter.
4. Heat 1 tablespoon of oil in the inner saucepan over a low-medium heat.
5. Brown half the meat balls and place them to one side.
6. Brown the other half of the meat balls and place them with the rest.
7. Add the other tablespoon of oil to the saucepan and brown the onions over a low heat for 2-3 minutes.
8. Add the garlic and celery and continue to cook for a few minutes until the onions start to clear and soften.
9. Add the zucchini and stir fry for a further minute.
10. Add the meat balls back into the saucepan and stir in the parsley.
11. Add the carbonara sauce and the stock.
12. Bring the mixture to the boil.
13. Turn down the heat and simmer gently for 3 minutes.
14. Add the pasta to the simmering sauce and continue to simmer a further minute with the lid on.
15. Turn off the heat and transfer the saucepan into the vacuum insulated outer container.
16. Close the lid and leave for a minimum of 1 hour.
17. Serve with grated cheese and a tossed green salad of your choice.

POACHED HERB CHICKEN

Serves 4–6

Ingredients

- 1 roasting chicken approximately 1 3/4 to 2 kg
- 1 cup assorted fresh herbs of your choice
- 1 tsp of olive oil
- 1 medium white onion, peeled and coarsely chopped
- 3 large carrots, peeled and cut into quarters
- 6 medium red potatoes, well scrubbed but not peeled
- 6 cups of chicken stock
- 1 tsp of salt
- 10 whole black peppercorns
- 2 cups of fresh green beans
- 1/4 of a cup of Dijon mustard
- 3 tbs of arrowroot

Method

1. Wash and dry the chicken, removing any visible fat. Stuff the cavity with the herbs and then put it in the refrigerator until ready to use.
2. Heat the inner cooking pot, add the oil and fry the onion for 3 minutes. Add the carrots and fry for 2 minutes.
3. Transfer the prepared chicken into the inner cooking pot, on top of the onions and carrots, and tuck the potatoes all around. Pour the stock over the chicken and vegetables and bring to a full boil.
4. Add the salt and peppercorns. Simmer for 15 minutes, skimming off any foam that rises to the surface.
5. Place the green beans on top of the chicken, cover, and place in the outer pot for 3 hours.
6. Just before serving, make a sauce: Take 3 cups of the stock from the chicken and pour it into a fat-strainer cup. When the fat has risen to the top, pour the defatted liquid into a saucepan. Remove 1/3 cup of the defatted stock and mix it with the arrowroot in a small bowl to make a paste. Stir the mustard into the saucepan and heat gently. Remove from the heat, stir in the paste, return to the heat and bring to a boil to thicken.
7. To serve: remove and thinly slice the chicken. Serve the meat with the potatoes and green beans, covered with the sauce.

CARIBBEAN CHICKEN & RICE

This is an ideal dish for a thermal cooker as everything can be prepared in the inner pot.

One pot meals such as this are ideal to cook in your motor home while you are on the move.

The use of chicken on the bone helps keep the chicken moist.

Ingredients

- 8 chicken pieces, 4 thighs, 4 drumsticks, skinned
- 1 tsp salt
- 1 tbs ground coriander
- 2 tsp ground cumin
- 1 tbs paprika
- 1/2 tsp ground nutmeg
- 1 chilli, seeded and chopped
- 1 onion, chopped
- 1 tsp fresh thyme
- 4 garlic cloves, crushed
- 2 tbs dark soy sauce
- juice of 1 lemon
- 2 tbs vegetable oil
- 2 tbs light muscovado sugar
- 350 gm long grain rice
- 3 tbs dark rum (optional)
- 410 gm tin black-eye beans, drained
- ground black pepper

To Marinade the Chicken

In a bowl mix together the ½ tsp of the salt, ½ tsp pepper, the coriander, cumin, paprika nutmeg the chilli, onion, thyme, garlic, the soy sauce and lemon juice.

Put the chicken pieces in a plastic food bag and add the contents of the bowl.

Work the marinade into the chicken pieces before sealing the bag and putting it in the fridge for 4 to 6 hours.

Method

1. Heat the vegetable oil and muscovado sugar in the inner pot until it turns a golden cover. Be careful not to over cook it or it will burn.
2. Put the chicken pieces in the inner pot saving the marinade.
3. Put on the lid and cook over a medium heat for 5 minutes, then turn the chicken and cook, covered, for another 5 minutes until evenly browned.
4. Stir in the onion and any remaining juices from the marinade.
5. Add the rice and beans.
6. Pour in 900 ml of water and the rum. Stir well and bring to the boil.
7. Turn down to a simmer and put on the lid. Simmer for 5 minutes.
8. Put the inner pot into the insulated outer container and shut the lid.
9. Thermal Cook without power for a minimum of 2 hours.
10. Check the seasoning before serving.

CHINESE LION'S HEAD MEATBALLS RECIPE

Ingredients

MEATBALLS

500 gm pound ground pork
2 tbs dried shrimp
1 tbs sliced ginger, minced
1 (8 oz) can water chestnuts, minced
1 scallions, finely sliced (including top) on the diagonal
1 egg, lightly beaten
1 tsp date palm sugar
1 tbs Shao Hsing wine or dry sherry
1 tbs soy sauce
1 tbs fresh minced garlic
2 ounces minced shiitake mushrooms
1½ tbs cornstarch
White pepper or Szechuan pepper to taste

CASSEROLE

3–4 tbs peanut oil for cooking
2 cup chicken stock
1 tsp ginger, minced
1 tsp garlic, minced
1 tsp sugar
1 tbs soy sauce
2 oz sliced shiitake mushrooms
2 tbs oyster sauce
500 gm bok choy, cut into bite-sized pieces

Method

1. Soak shrimps in warm water for 30 minutes then drain and mince.
2. Mix the minced shrimps with the remaining meatball ingredients. Set aside for 30 minutes in the fridge.
3. Form the mixture into 4 large meatballs and roll in cornstarch and flatten them slightly.
4. Heat the oil in the inner pot and when hot add the meatballs.
5. Brown each side of the meatballs.
6. Once brown remove the meatballs with a slotted spoon and drain on paper towels.
7. Pour off any oil left in the inner pot and then add the chicken stock, ginger, garlic, sugar, soy sauce, shiitake mushrooms and oyster sauce.
8. Bring to the boil
9. Add the meatballs and bring back to the boil.
10. Simmer for 5 minutes before putting on the lid, turn off the heat and place the inner pot into the insulated outer container.
11. Shut the lid and leave to thermal cook for 2 hours. Slightly longer will not hurt.
12. Before serving remove the inner pot from the outer container.
13. Carefully take out the meatballs and put them somewhere to keep warm.
14. Bring the inner pot to the boil, and then turn off the heat.
15. Arrange the bok choy in bowls and place a meatball on top.
16. Pour over the stock and serve with a separate bowl of steamed rice which could be cooked in a top pot for the Thermal Cooker.

CHINESE LION'S HEAD MEATBALLS

STOVE TOP TIME: 5 MINUTES

SHUTTLE CHEF TIME: 60 MINUTES MINIMUM

Lion's head is a dish from the Huaiyang cuisine of Eastern China, consisting of large pork meatballs stewed with vegetables.

The name derives from the shape of the meatball which is supposed to resemble the head of the lion and the cabbage (or other vegetables), which is supposed to resemble the lion's mane.

The dish originated in the region of Yangzhou and Zhenjiang in Jiangsu province, with the plain variety more common in Yangzhou and the red variety more common in Zhenjiang. The dish became a part of Shanghai cuisine with the influx of migrants in the 19th and early 20th century.

SOURCE OF INFORMATION WIKIPEDIA

PORK STANDING RIB ROAST IN APPLE SAUCE

STOVE TOP TIME: 25-30 MINUTES

SHUTTLE CHEF TIME: 3 HOURS MINIMUM

Ingredients

1–1.5 kg standing pork rib roast
3 medium potatoes, halved
2 medium carrots, peeled and cut into chunks
1 large onion, peeled and cut into quarters
1 small sweet potato, peeled and cut into chunks
100 gm of fresh green beans, top/tailed and cut in half
1 packet of dried peas
360 gm jar of apple sauce
Enough unsweetened apple juice to cover the ingredients
Salt and Pepper to taste

Method

1. Brown the standing rib roast all over to provide colour and reduce the fat.
2. Stand the rib roast up in the middle of the 4.5 litre inner saucepan.
3. Surround with the chunky vegetables and dried peas.
4. Pour in the apple sauce and enough unsweetened apple juice to cover the ingredients.
5. Bring to the boil and simmer with the lid on for a minimum of 25 to 30 minutes.
6. *NOTE:* If you are using the two 3 litre inner saucepans you can lay the rib roast down with the dried peas, onions, apple sauce and juice and then place all of the other vegetables in the second saucepan and cover with water, bring this to the boil and simmering for 8 to 10 minutes.
7. Place the inner saucepan into the outer container and close the lid.
8. Leave this meal for a minimum of 3 hours.
9. To serve, remove the roast and vegetables and vigorously boil the remaining liquid to reduce by a half.
10. Pour this gravy over the individual servings.

PASTA BAKE

There is no need to precook the pasta in this dish.

Ingredients

500 gm of beef meat balls
(or make your own...see recipe below)
2 tbs of oil
2 onions coarsely chopped
2 cloves of garlic crushed
1 stick of celery sliced
1 cup of sliced mushrooms
1 x 750 mL jar of pasta sauce
750 mL of water
salt and pepper to taste
good pinch of mixed herbs
1/2 cup of chopped fresh parsley
1 1/2 cups of penne pasta
grated cheese to serve.

Method

1. Heat 1 tbs of oil in the inner saucepan over a low–medium heat.
2. Brown half the meat balls and place them to one side.
3. Brown the other half and place these with the others.
4. Add the other tablespoon of oil to the saucepan and brown the onions over a low heat for 2–3 minutes.
5. Add the garlic and celery and continue to cook for a few minutes or until the onions start to turn clear and soften.
6. Add in the mushrooms and stir fry a further minute.
7. Add the meat balls back into the pot and stir in the pasta sauce and water.
8. Bring the mixture to the boil.
9. Turn down the heat and simmer for 3 minutes adding in herbs.
10. Add the pasta to the simmering sauce.
11. Place the lid on and continue to simmer a further minute.
12. Turn off the heat and transfer the saucepan into the vacuum insulated outer container.
13. Close the lid and leave for a minimum of 1 hour.
14. Stir in parsley and serve with grated cheese and tossed green salad of your choice.

TO MAKE YOUR OWN MEAT BALLS

400 gm of minced steak
1 clove of garlic
1 egg
1 tbs of flour
salt and pepper to taste

1. Mix all of the ingredients together.
2. Seperate out into small portions.
3. Roll each of the portions into balls approximately 2 cm in diameter.

MADRAS LAMB CURRY

STOVE TOP TIME: 12 MINUTES

SHUTTLE CHEF TIME: 2 HOURS MINIMUM

This recipe is really easy and the ideal meal to make when you are on the road. It comes from a very old book that I have, produced by Bisto and uses bisto gravy powder. I have used granules as they are easier and were all I had in the cupboard.

Ingredients

- 3 tbs of vegetable oil
- 1 large onion, chopped
- 1 green pepper, deseeded and chopped
- 2 chillies, deseeded and finely chopped. Use less if you don't want it too hot
- 2 garlic cloves, crushed
- 2 tbs of Madras curry powder
- 500 gm of lamb shoulder, cut into cubes
- 3 tsp of Bisto or other gravy powder
- 500 mL of water
- 2 tbs tomato puree
- Juice of 1 lemon

Method

1. Put the inner pot on a medium heat and add the oil.
2. When the oil is up to temperature (not too hot) add the onion, green pepper, chillies and garlic. Cook for about 4 minutes until the onion just starts to soften.
3. Add the curry powder and cook for 2–3 minutes stirring all the time to stop it sticking to the base of the pot.
4. Add the meat and keep moving it around until it starts to brown.
5. Mix the Bisto with a little water to make a smooth cream. You won't have to do this if you are using granules.
6. Add the rest of the water, tomato puree and lemon juice to the inner pot and stir well.
7. Stir in the Bisto and bring to the boil.
8. Simmer for 5 minutes with the lid on.
9. Put the inner pot into the insulated outer container.
10. Leave to thermal cook for at least 2 hours. Longer will be better.
11. Check seasoning and adjust before serving with rice and Nan bread.

SIMPLE LAMB OR BEEF STEW

Serves 6

Ingredients

- 1 kg of lamb or beef cubed into large pieces
- 2 tbs of plain flour
- 1 tbs of olive oil
- 2 large onions cut into quarters
- 2 cloves of garlic crushed
- 1 stalk of celery sliced into medium pieces
- 1 parsnip cubed into small pieces
- 1/2 a swede turnip cubed into small pieces
- 1 packet of dried green peas
- 1 Massel vegetable stock cube.
- 2 tbs of soy sauce
- 1/2 a cup of barley
- 3 cups of water.

Salt and pepper to taste.

You can vary this to suit your tastes by the following: -

- Add some mixed herbs, either dried or fresh.
- With the beef you can substitute one cup of water for a cup of red wine.
- You may add two table spoons of Thai red curry paste.
- You may also add a tin of Tomatoes however you will need to adjust the water amount to compensate.
- You may also substitute frozen vegetables for the fresh mentioned above.

Method

1. Heat the oil in the inner pot and cook the onions and garlic over a medium heat until they are transparent.
2. Remove the pot from the heat.
3. Toss the cubed meat in seasoned flour.
4. Add the vegetables, soy sauce and water to the pot with the cooked onions and garlic.
5. Bring to the boil over medium heat, and then add meat, barley, stock cube and dried peas.
6. Bring the contents to the boil and then reduce the heat to a slow simmer for 12 to 15 minutes with the lid on, stirring occasionally.
7. Transfer to outer pot for 3-4 hours. Can be left up to 8 hours.

RABBIT IN RED WINE

Ingedients

- 1.5 kg of prepared rabbit pieces
- 1 tbs of plain flour
- 2 tbs of olive oil
- 2 onions cut into quarters
- 100 gm of bacon chopped
- 2 cloves of garlic crushed
- 1 stalk of celery finely chopped
- 1 carrot diced
- 1 potato diced
- 1 bay leaf
- 2 sprigs of thyme
- 1 cup of sliced mushrooms
- 1 cup of red wine
- 1 cup of chicken stock
- Salt and freshly ground black pepper
- 2 tbs chopped fresh parsley

Method

1. Toss the rabbit pieces in the flour.
2. Heat 1 tablespoon of oil over medium heat.
3. Add the rabbit pieces and brown all over and then remove them.
4. Lower the heat and add the remaining oil.
5. Add the onions and fry until softened.
6. Add the celery and garlic and cook for 2–3 minutes.
7. Add the carrots and potatoes, bay leaf and thyme and stir fry a further 2–3 minutes.
8. Return the rabbit pieces to the pot with the mushrooms, wine, stock, salt and pepper to taste.
9. Stir together and bring slowly to the boil.
10. Simmer gently for 10 minutes stirring occasionally.
11. Turn off the heat and transfer the inner saucepan into the insulated outer container.
12. Close the lid and leave for 3 hours minimum.
13. Serve sprinkled with chopped parsley.

PROSCIUTTO WITH PINE NUT RISOTTO

SHUTTLE CHEF TIME:
2-3
HOURS MINIMUM

Not your average Risotto......
no more stirring for 40 minutes
while the wine is absorbed.

Using the Shuttle Chef a Risotto
can be completed in minutes.

Ingedients

- 2 large onions chopped
- 4 cloves of garlic crushed
- 1 stick of celery sliced
- 1-2 tbs of olive oil
- 1 cup of arborio rice
- 1/4 of a cup of white wine
- 2 cups of hot chicken stock
- 1/4 of a tsp of dried thyme
- Salt and pepper to taste

ADDITIONS

- 1 tbs of butter cut into small pieces
- 1/2 a cup of grated parmesan cheese
- 4 slices of prosciutto cut into small squares
- 1/2 a cup of toasted pine nuts
- 1/2 a cup of finely chopped parsley

ALTERNATIVELY

You could replace the additions with a variety of fillings of your choice

Method

1. Saute the onions in oil over a low-medium heat for 2–3 minutes.
2. Add the celery and garlic and continue to saute a further minute until the onion starts to soften.
3. Add the rice and continue to saute for a further minute.
4. Stir in the wine, stirring any bits caught on the bottom of the saucepan.
5. Stir in the hot stock and add the thyme, salt and pepper.
6. Bring the mixture back to the boil whilst stirring.
7. Turn down the heat to a simmer and close the lid.
8. Simmer for 1 minute.
9. Turn off the heat and transfer the saucepan into the vacuum insulated outer container.
10. Close the lid and leave for a minimum of 3/4 of an hour.
11. Open the lid of the saucepan and stir in the butter.
12. Stir in the parmesan, prosciutto, pine nuts and parsley, leaving a little of each to serve as a garnish.
13. Close the lid and leave it in the outer container for a further 5 minutes before serving.
14. Serve and garnish with the left over additives.
15. Serve with a fresh tossed green salad of your choice.

CHRISTMAS PUDDING

Ingredients

150 gm of raisins chopped (1 cup)
100 gm of sultanas (3/4 of a cup)
100 gm of currants (3/4 of a cup)
75 gm of pitted dates chopped (1/2 a cup)
75 gm of figs or prunes chopped (1/2 a cup)
1/3 of a cup of brandy or whisky

125 gm of Tandaco suet mix
1/4 of a cup of plain flour
1 cup of fresh bread crumbs
A pinch of salt
1 tsp of mixed spice
1/2 a tsp of ground ginger
3/4 of a cup of dark brown sugar
2 eggs lightly beaten
1/4 of a cup of lime marmalade
1/4 of a tsp of soda bicarb
1 tbs of boiling water

Method

1. Combine the dried fruit in a bowl.
2. Heat the brandy (whisky) in a saucepan over a medium heat until hot but do not bring to the boil.
3. Remove from the heat and pour over the fruit mix.
4. Stir to combine.
5. Cover and leave to soak at room temperature overnight.
6. Cut two circles of baking paper to fit the pudding or cake tin. (one for the base and one for the top)
7. Grease the basin and line the base.
8. Make a pleat in a sheet of alfoil, large enough to cover the top of the basin with atleast a 3 cm overhang.
9. Take a length of alfoil about 50 cm long, fold into 4 lengthways to make a strap for lifting the pudding basin in and out. (If this seems to be too much effort then make it in our cake/pudding tin.....you just wont have the traditional pudding shape)
10. Combine the dry ingredients, except for the soda bicarb, in a bowl.
11. Stir through the fruit mix, then add the eggs and soda bicarb (dissolved in boiling water)
12. Mix thoroughly together until well combined.
13. Spoon into the pudding basin and place a circle of baking paper on top of the mix.
14. Place the pleated alfoil on the top of the basin with the pleat running through the centre.
15. Secure the alfoil with string.
16. Place a suitable sized trivet or pad of alfoil (for the 3 litre) in the base of the inner saucepan and add enough boiling water to come 2/3 the way up the sides of the basin.
17. Lower the pudding basin into the boiling water (using the alfoil strap)
18. Bring the water back to the boil.
19. Turn down the heat and simmer gently for 45 minutes with the lid on.
20. Check regularly and add more boiling water if necessary to make sure that the level is topped up to that 2/3 the way up the sides of the basin.
21. Turn off the heat and transfer the inner saucepan into the vacuum insulated outer container.
22. Close the lid and leave for a minimum of 8 hours.
23. Test with a skewer, which should come out clean.
24. If not then return it to a simmer on the stove top for another 20 minutes.
25. Place the saucepan back into the Shuttle Chef for 2 more hours.
26. Allow to cool in the basin.

CHRISTMAS PUDDING

PREPARATION TIME: 30 MINUTES

STOVE TOP TIME: 65 MINUTES

SHUTTLE CHEF TIME: 8 HOURS MINIMUM

This is the traditional Christmas pudding but prepared and cooked in the Shuttle Chef.
It couldn't be easier and the results are always so moist.
No more boiling for hours, checking water levels and worrying about water getting into the cloth etc.
Such an efficient time and energy saver........you could make these on a more regular basis as the effort is far less than the reward.

Serves: 6
(made in a 1 litre pudding basin or suitable tin)

Suitable for the 3 or 4.5 litre inner saucepans
(Using our stainless steel cake/steamed pudding tin or any suitably shaped 16 cm steamed pudding tin)

CHRISTMAS CAKE

Ingredients

150 gm of raisins chopped (1 cup)
100 gm of sultanas (3/4 of a cup)
100 gm of currants (3/4 of a cup)
75 gm of pitted dates chopped (1/2 a cup)
75 gm of figs or prunes chopped (1/2 a cup)
50 gm of glazed cherries chopped (1/2 a cup)
1/2 a cup of brandy or whisky
125 gm of butter (room temperature)
100 gm dark brown sugar (1/2 a cup)
1 tbs of treacle
1 tsp of finely grated orange rind
2 eggs
1 cup of plain flour
1/4 of a cup of self raising flour
2 tsp of ground cardamom
1 tsp of nutmeg
1/2 a cup of slivered almonds toasted
Whole blanched almonds toasted for decorating

Method

1. Combine the dried fruit in a bowl.
2. Heat the brandy (whisky) in a saucepan over a medium heat until hot but do not bring to the boil.
3. Remove from the heat and pour over the fruit mix.
4. Stir to combine.
5. Cover and leave to stand at room temperature overnight for soaking.
6. Cut two circles of baking paper to fit the cake tin.
7. Grease the cake tin and line the base with one of the baking paper circles.
8. Beat the butter, sugar, treacle and orange rind in a bowl until smooth.
9. Add the eggs, 1 at a time, beating well after each addition.
10. Add the flour and spices and fold to combine.
11. Stir in the fruit mixture and slivered almonds.
12. Spoon into the cake tin and smooth the surface.
13. Decorate with toasted whole almonds.
14. Cover with the other baking paper circle.
15. Put the lid onto the cake tin and clip down (If using another cake tin, cover with alfoil and tie securely with string)
16. Add enough boiling water to the inner saucepan to come 2/3 rds the way up the sides of the cake tin.
17. if you are using the 4.5 litre saucepan, place a suitable trivet inside first.
18. If you are using the 3 litre saucepan, place a fold of alfoil in the base.
19. Lower the cake tin into the boiling water (using the handles or an alfoil strap)
20. Bring the water back to the boil.
21. Turn down the heat to a low simmer.
22. Simmer gently with the lid on for 65–70 minutes, adding more boiling water if necessary.
23. Top up the boiling water to 2/3 rds just before transferring the saucepan into the Shuttle Chef.
24. Turn off the heat and transfer the saucepan into the vacuum insulated outer container.
25. Close the lid and leave for a minimum of 8 hours or even overnight.
26. Test with a skewer which should come out clean.
27. If the skewer is not clean you can return the saucepan to a simmer on the stove top for another 20 minutes and then place it back in the vacuum insulated outer for another two hours.
28. Allow to cool in the tin

CHRISTMAS CAKE

PREPARATION TIME: 30 MINUTES

STOVE TOP TIME: 65 MINUTES

SHUTTLE CHEF TIME: 8 HOURS MINIMUM

This is the traditional Christmas or Festival Cake but prepared and cooked in the Shuttle Chef.
It couldn't be easier and the results are always so moist.
Such an efficient time and energy saver........you could make these on a regular basis as the effort is far less than the reward.

Suitable for the 3 or 4.5 litre inner saucepans

(Using our stainless steel cake/steamed pudding tin or any suitable 16 cm cake tin)

Serves: 10

(This recipe can be doubled to make two cakes or 1 cake and 1 pudding)

Barbecues & Grills

Barbecues and grills have been the main style of cooking in the Australian bush for decades. There are literally a dozen different ways to barbecue when outdoors and on the move. These range from using a cooking fire and coals to many of the compact portable grills that use LP gas as a fuel source. In addition, there are barbecues that utilise other fuel sources such as heat beads and fuel spirit.

GAS AND OTHER FUEL STOVES

There is a huge range of portable gas and fuel stoves and portable barbecues available in the marketplace today. Typically they come in a 2 to 4 burner styles with most having folding or removable legs and pack away easily for travelling on the road. When purchasing, consider looking for a model that includes a steel plate and perhaps a griddle plate for grilling and cooking everything from toast to steak.

A number of manufacturers also produce similar units that will run on fuel spirit instead of LP gas. These should be an option on extended trips when it is impossible to get a gas bottle filled on your chosen route.

FACT BOX

To calculate how long you will get from a gas bottle.

For an average two burner fuel stove (13,000 BTU) – at flat out will run for about 2 hours on a 1.65 litre fuel tank.

The Coleman company is the best in this category and produces a number of models that will run on shellite and ULP. When using fuel stoves always filter the fuel when you fill the tank and always carry a spare generator.

OPEN FIRE AND COALS

It's traditional that Australian's on the road use an open fire to cook their meals. Although cooking on the open fire binds us to our historic roots, the use of fire in the bush must be considered carefully. With concerns about bush fires nowadays there are obviously many restrictions placed on where, when and how one can use an open fire to cook in the bush. Where restrictions enable the use of fire, campfire cooking in the bush continues to be one of the most pleasing ways to cook meals on the road.

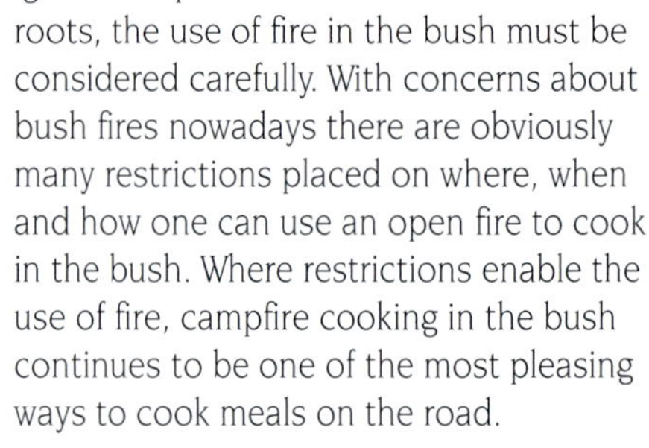

A good cooking fire takes time to establish and bush cooks should allow at least an hour. For many it is one of the highlights of the day on the road. To establish a good fire you'll need a supply

FACT BOX

CONTROLLING HEAT

You can actually control the temperature of a campfire! This is done by controlling the amount of coals on a particular section of the fire.

***Low heat** – Just single coals on the ground – outside area of the coal bed.*

***Medium Heat** – Low flame area, good well-established coal bed.*

***High Heat** – Middle of the fire and the deepest section of the coal bed.*

FACT BOX

TOTAL FIRE BANS

Firstly it is everyone's responsibility to be aware that a Total Fire Ban has been declared.

On days of Total Fire Ban it is illegal to have any open flame in the outdoors (including tents, trailers and vehicles) – including campfires, portable gas or liquid fuelled stoves and gas lights. With recent changes to legislation around Australia everyone should check the up to date regulations before leaving one state and moving to the next. The fines involved are serious, not to mention the other consequences.

of kindling, a larger supply of small, branch timber or split logs and ideally a number of larger, dry logs or even split logs. These larger pieces are what will generate the coals.

Check that it is legal to collect firewood in your camping area—soft woods burn quickly and produce ashes (not ideal)—hard woods burn more slowly and produce coals—ideal.

Start your fire with kindling using the time honoured tepee method and ignite with newspaper (or some now prefer to use a couple of fire lighters). As the fire becomes established, add larger and medium pieces maintaining the tepee formation. Always remember to keep the fire well oxygenated. Lastly add the largest timber and then allow the logs to burn to coals. Once the fire is reduced to coals, flatten them to make a bed or layer of heat on which to cook.

OPEN FIRE GRILLS AND ACCESSORIES

There is a range of cooking accessories produced in Australia for use on the open fire. However, there are three essential styles to cook with:

- Large handled steel or Hillbilly frypan
- Barbecue swing grill or grill on folding legs (often called a metal fire grate)
- Barbecue swing hot plate or hot plate with folding legs

Using either one or all three you can prepare almost any meal with ease on the open fire.

The best material is ordinary heavy Australian steel, but there are options in stainless steel and cast iron.

Items that travellers should also consider having include a billy, long handled saucepan, long handled barbecue utensils and a trivet to suspend your billy over the fire without being in contact with the actual fire.

Other items that are occasionally useful are skewers, roast rack, grill brush, meat thermometer, basting brush, jaffle iron, metal shields and heat resistant gloves.

GRILLED SALMON STEAKS WITH GINGER VINAIGRETTE

PREPARATION TIME: 10 MINUTES

COOKING TIME: 10 MINUTES

Ingredients

4 salmon steaks, about 150–200 gm each
salt and black pepper to taste
2 tbs olive oil

VINAIGRETTE

Ginger Vinaigrette (pp 59)
1 small shallot, finely chopped
6 tbs olive or vegetable oil
lemon or lime juice to taste

Method

1. Preheat the hot plate to medium-high. Coat salmon with oil and season lightly. Grill 3–5 minutes on each side until lightly browned and just cooked through.
2. Meanwhile, make the vinaigrette. Mix together the vinaigrette, shallots, oil and lemon/lime juice, then season to taste. Spoon over the salmon steaks.

SESAME BARBECUED PRAWNS

PREPARATION TIME: 20 MINUTES

COOKING TIME: 5 MINUTES

Ingredients

- 1 kg large prawns
- ¼ cup olive oil
- ¼ red or white wine
- 4 shallots, finely chopped
- 1 tsp grated lemon zest
- ½ tsp cracked black peppercorns
- 12 bamboo skewers, pre-soaked in water
- ½ cup sesame seeds

Method

1. Peel and de-vein prawns. Leave the shell on the tail end.
2. Combine oil, wine, shallots, lemon zest and pepper. Mix well.
3. Thread the prawns onto bamboo skewers (about 4 per skewer) so that they can lay flat.
4. Place the skewers in a shallow dish and pour the marinade over.
5. Toast the sesame seeds in frypan.
6. Sprinkle the toasted sesame seeds over prawns each side, pressing then on well. Refrigerate for about 30 minutes.
7. Place on the hotplate until opaque.

SOY CHICKEN WINGS

PREPARATION TIME:
6
MINUTES

COOKING TIME:
10-15
MINUTES

Ingredients

2 kg chicken wings
Honey Glaze (pp 61)
3 tbs soy sauce

Method

1. Add soy sauce to the Honey Glaze and marinate the wings, covered in the refrigerator for at least 1 hour.
2. Heat the barbecue to a medium heat. Place wings on a flat grill. Turn and brush the wings frequently with glaze until they are brown and crisp.

As an alternative, toast 3 tablespoons sesame seeds, stirring for 30 seconds then sprinkle over wings.

WARM CHICKEN SALAD

PREPARATION TIME: 5 MINUTES

COOKING TIME: 15 MINUTES

Ingredients

- 4 chicken breasts
- Green Rub (pp 58)
- 1 tsp oil
- 1 red pepper, cut into strips
- 1 green pepper, cut into strips
- 1 eggplant, sliced lengthways
- 1 Spanish onion, cut into rings
- ½ lettuce, shredded

DRESSING

- ½ cup olive oil
- ¼ cup red wine vinegar
- 1 tbs Green Rub (pp 58)

Method

1. Flatten chicken breasts slightly to even thickness and slice into strips. Mix Green Rub and oil together and rub well into the chicken. Cover and stand 1 hour in refrigerator.
2. Heat the barbecue to medium-high and oil hotplate and grill bars. Place chicken on grill and cook 6 minutes each side. Place vegetables (except lettuce) on the hotplate, drizzle with oil and cook for 5 minutes, turning to cook through. Place a bed of lettuce onto individual plates and place barbecued vegetables in the centre. Cut the chicken into thin slices and arrange on vegetables.
3. Mix dressing ingredients together and pour over chicken and warm salad. Serve with crusty bread.

SOUTHERN BARBECUED CHICKEN BREASTS

PREPARATION TIME: 5 MINUTES

COOKING TIME: 20 MINUTES

Ingredients

1 portion of Secret Marinade (pp 60)
1 cup cider vinegar
1/3 cup Worcestershire sauce
2 tbs French-style mustard

1 kg fresh chicken breasts cut into large pieces

Method

1. Prepare Secret Marinade (pp 60).
2. Place chicken in marinade for 1 hour.
3. Heat barbecue to moderate and oil the grill plate. Lightly sear chicken pieces on all sides over direct heat.
4. Brush chicken with marinade and lower heat. Cook covered with foil, turning 3–4 times until chicken is cooked through, allow to rest.
5. Heat any leftover marinade and pour over chicken to serve. Eat with rice and a green salad.

BARBECUED CHICKEN AND MUSHROOM PATTIES

PREPARATION TIME: 10 MINUTES

COOKING TIME: 20 MINUTES

Ingredients

500 kg minced chicken
½ cup dried breadcrumbs
1 medium onion, finely chopped
2 tbs chopped parsley
¼ cup mushrooms, finely chopped
1 egg
vegetable oil

Method

1. Mix all ingredients except oil. Knead with one hand to make mixture fine in texture. Shapc into flat patties.
2. Heat barbecue or grill to medium. Oil the grill bars. Place patties on grill. Cook for 10 minutes on each side until cooked through.
3. Serve hot with cold green salad and potato salad.

SUCCULENT PORK TENDERS

Ingredients

½ cup soy sauce
¼ cup sesame oil
¼ cup brown vinegar
fresh ginger, minced
1 bunch coriander, finely chopped
2 tbs crushed garlic
2 tbs brown sugar
½ cup water
1.5 kg pork tenderloins
oil for grill

Method

1. Mix all ingredients except pork thoroughly. Add pork and marinate in fridge overnight.
2. Place pork on hot grill or barbecue for 6 minutes each side. Baste with marinade and turn frequently so as not to burn.
3. Allow to rest. Serve with rice and salad.

GLAZED PORK
SPARE RIBS

PREPARATION TIME: 10 MINUTES

COOKING TIME: 35 MINUTES

Ingredients

1 kg pork spare ribs (American-Style)
Honey Glaze (pp 61)
2 tbs soy sauce

Method

1. Mix Honey Glaze and soy sauce.
2. Cover ribs both side generously with marinade. Leave in refrigerator for 2 hours.
3. Wrap ribs individually in foil and place on barbecue (medium–hot) for 10 minutes each side. Turn over twice.
4. Remove ribs from foil and brown on barbecue for 5 minutes each side. Allow to rest.

SATAY LAMB SKEWERS

PREPARATION TIME: 10 MINUTES

COOKING TIME: 15 MINUTES

Ingredients

¼ cup peanut butter
¼ tsp chilli powder or Tabasco sauce
¼ tsp ground ginger
Juice of one lemon
¾ cup canola oil
1 tbs brown sugar
1 kg boned shoulder of lamb
12 bamboo skewers pre-soaked in ice water

Method

1. Mix all ingredients for marinade in a bowl.
2. Cut lamb into 2 cm cubes and place into marinade for 1 hour. Reserve some marinade for pouring over cooked skewers.
3. Heat barbecue grill to medium-hot.
4. Thread lamb onto skewers.
5. Cook skewered meat on grill barbecue for 12-15 minutes until cooked through and brown, turning frequently.
6. Serve with rice or as finger food.

CHILLI CUTLETS

PREPARATION TIME: 5 MINUTES

COOKING TIME: 10 MINUTES

Ingredients

500 gm lamb chops (about 12)
60 gm butter
Chilli sauce (see page 62)
1 tbs olive oil

Method

1. Bring butter to room temperature. Mix softened butter with chilli sauce.
2. Trim off any excess fat leaving just the meaty part.
3. Take half the chilli mixture and rub over the cutlets.
4. Cook cutlets on a hotplate or grill 3–4 minutes each side.
5. When cooked, remove cutlets and rub some of the remaining chilli butter on each chop to serve.
6. Serve with salad and chips.

WARM BEEF SALAD

PREPARATION TIME: 10 MINUTES

COOKING TIME: 10-15 MINUTES

Ingredients

- 2 thick scotch fillet or porterhouse steaks approx. 300 gm each
- 1 clove garlic crushed
- 1 green chilli chopped (or more if you prefer)
- 2 tbs oil

SALAD

Baby spinach leaves & rocket lettuce
Finely sliced Beetroot
Cherry tomatoes
Kalamata olives
Salad dressing

Method

1. Mix garlic, chilli and oil with salt and pepper to taste. Place in bowl with steaks for 30–60 minutes.
2. Heat frypan or hotplate to very hot. Sear steaks on both sides.
3. Reduce heat and cook for further 3 minutes each side.
4. Remove steak and rest it while you mix all salad ingredients.
5. Cut meat into thin slices and arrange on a plate with salad. Serve warm..

GOURMET RISSOLES

PREPARATION TIME: 15 MINUTES

COOKING TIME: 20 MINUTES

Ingredients

500 gm coarsely minced steak
150 gm finely diced mushrooms
One large onion finely chopped
1 cup breadcrumbs
1 tbs plum or tomato sauce
½ tsp dried mixed herbs
1 tsp honey
½ tsp tabasco sauce
2 eggs

1 cup of breadcrumbs for coating
Plus your choice of fillings for hamburger, tomato, lettuce, bacon, beetroot etc

Method

1. Mix all rissole ingredients together.
2. Form into patties and roll in breadcrumbs.
3. Grill on a medium-hot barbecue about 15 minutes until cooked.
4. Serve in a hamburger bun or between two slices of lightly toasted Vienna loaf.

KANGAROO STEAK

PREPARATION TIME: 2 MINUTES

COOKING TIME: 10 MINUTES

Ingredients

500 gm Kangaroo Fillets
125 mL Barbecue Sauce or a Red Wine Marinade (pp 60)
2 tablespoons of Olive Oil

Method

1. Place the Kangaroo fillets into a mix of the oil and the BBQ sauce for around an hour.
2. Heat your pan or hot plate to a medium to hot level.
3. Turn the pan down to medium and then add the Kangaroo, allow excess marinade to drain off before cooking, turn after sealing one side.
4. Cook on one side for around 3–5 minutes and then turn over and cook for another 5 minutes, some part of the fillet maybe a lot thicker than the rest so use your judgement. Turn the heat off and allow the Kangaroo to rest. Kangaroo is best eaten medium-rare.
5. Serve with mashed potato and vegetable skewers, you can re-use the marinade as a sauce if you simmer it in a pan first.

VEGETABLE SKEWERS

Serves 2

PREPARATION TIME: 10 MINUTES

COOKING TIME: 15 MINUTES

Ingredients

½ Red pepper
½ Green pepper
½ Medium onion
1 small zucchini
1 large clove of garlic sliced across in rings
oil spray
Aluminium foil
4 Bamboo skewers (pre-soaked in water)

Method

1. Slice the vegetables into bite size pieces.
2. Arrange on the skewers alternately with a slice of garlic in between each set of vegetables.
3. Spray with oil and season lightly with salt and pepper.
4. Place on a medium to hot pan or hot plate and place a sheet of foil over the top to retain the heat and the moisture, cook for around 15 minutes turning occasionally.

CHOCOLATE SCRAMBLED EGGS

PREPARATION TIME: 3 MINUTES

COOKING TIME: 3 MINUTES

Ingredients

6 fresh eggs
50 mL thickened cream
100 gm of dark or milk chocolate
1 tbs of butter

Method

1. Beat the eggs and the cream in a bowl with a pinch of salt.
2. Melt the butter in a frypan or on a hot plate, moderate heat.
3. Gently pour the egg mix into the pan and using a spatula move it around until it has just started to cook.
4. Toss the chocolate broken into squares into the egg mix, it will start to melt almost immediately.
5. Using the spatula mix the melted chocolate into the uncooked scrambled eggs.
6. As it mixes the egg will change colour. Remove the eggs from the pan just as it starts to look cooked.
7. You may like to serve it on pancakes or waffles.

Misty Gully Smokehouse

To many of us the aroma and taste of a summers night meal cooked on the family wood fired BBQ are some of our fondest memories. You can conjour up those memories and tastes easily by adding a little or a lot of smoke to your cooking.

Traditionally, the addition of smoke was a necessity along with lots of salt for the preservation of food, now a days it is all about the flavour and the journey.

Like the BBQ, the fish smoker or smokehouse has become the domain of many men, some go to great lengths to build a purpose built smoke house in the back yard or sit beside a small metal box fuelled by burners only to find that the time ans effort needed to maintain a reliable constant temperature is more of a chore than a pleasant past time.

Retirement is about sitting back and smelling the roses or smoke in this instance and that is why many have resorted to removing the chance of failure by investing in an electric smoker. Using one of these versatile pieces of equipment is so easy and you can pretty much guarantee success due to the amount of control over your slow cook.

Turn it on, put in the wood, place your meat or fish on the shelves, close the door and sit back with your beer or wine and enjoy the aroma as it slowly escapes into the air around you.

One smoker of choice is the Masterbuilt Electric Smoker. It is a versatile outdoor cooker and you don't have to add smoke at all if you don't want to. It can be used for making damper to slow cooking roasts to smoking up a storm. The digital timer and thermostat with the fully insulated body is perfect for those of us who like the set and forget type of cooker. The consistant gentle temperature that you can only get with electricity means that failures are very rare and there is no more having to constantly check if the heat beads in the BBQ Kettle are still burning or if the temperature has risen up too high in the gas BBQ.

THE OPTIONS

When smoking fish and chicken the first question that often comes to mind is to brine or not to brine. Brining does make a moister flesh and reduces the chance of a bland dry result. You can smoke most any food including meats and vegetables.

For those of you that do not have a full understanding of the smoking process you do need to understand what you are trying to achieve and the different smoking processes that are available. The following will give you a brief overview of the 3 main processes.

ADDING SMOKEY FLAVOUR TO BBQ OR CAMP OVEN

1. Smoking simply to cook your food and add a smokey flavour for immediate consumption **(Hot Smoked)**

Use this method for fish fillets or for an easy no maintenance way to cook a steak, chicken fillets, roasts, ribs or sausages. Generally don't use a brine when cooking fish or chicken this way but do soak them in a seasoned mix that you would consider to be more of a marinade than a brine. Your favourite sauce or marinade or a pre prepared dry seasoning mix blended with a little water and oil is perfect for all meats. Marinate your roast overnight, put it in the smoker in the morning, turn it on for a slow cook and it will be ready for dinner that night.

TRUE HOT SMOKING

2. Smoking your meats to extend its shelf/fridge life, can be eaten immediately or refrigerated or frozen in a vacuum sealed bag or air tight container **(Hot Smoked)**

You can smoke fish like trout or salmon to extend their fridge life and definitely use a brine in these instances, there are many recipes on the internet or you can buy a pre mix that includes nitrites to assist with the curing process. The addition of the nitrites aids in the absorption of the smokey flavour and gives you the added protection from potential bacteria that the meat may pick up during the longer preparation and pre cooking stages of curing 4hrs, soaking in fresh clean water 2 hours, air drying in a refrigerator 1hour, smoking 1 hour. You will also find that brining will improve the texture and moisture level of the flesh. The soaking step is to remove any excess salts from the flesh, a little tip is to slice off a little piece of the flesh after the soaking stage and cook it lightly in the microwave. If it is still too salty return it to fresh water and soak a little longer.

This process will take approximately 8 hours from kitchen to plate.

Also use this process for semi dried sausages like kransky, chorizo, kabana or bratwurst and for bacon and ham not to mention sandwich meats like pastrami and smoked chicken etc. Making your own sausages and bacon/ham is a lot easier these days thanks to pre mixes now being made available to the public. See *www.mistygully.com.au* for more details on cures, pre-mixes and sausage casings etc.

TRUE COLD SMOKING

3. Smoking your meats as part of a curing process, best for later consumption or storage in your fridge **(Cold Smoked)**

This process would be used for fish like salmon that is effectively intended to be eaten raw, like sushi or for continental meats like prosciutto, salamis and of course traditional bacon and ham. You can use a home made brine mix or a commercial pre mix that contains all required ingredients including nitrites to provide the added anti bacterial protection and improved curing. The procedure for curing salmon/bacon involves the flesh being cured (the chemicals in the salts basically cooks the flesh) in the brine for an extended period 8-12hrs, then being soaked in fresh clean water to remove any excess salts 5hrs, then air dried in a refrigerated environment to eliminate excess surface moisture 12hrs, then cold smoked without the use of any heat for 5 hours plus. Cold smoking is performed in a room temperature environment that obtains its smoke without heat from an external source. The air must be circulating around the meat and the temperature must be consistent and the correct humidity.

This process can take days.

THE FOLLOWING RECIPES IN THIS BOOK ARE FOR TRUE HOT SMOKING ONLY.

HOW LONG

One of the most frequent questions is "How do you know when your meat is cooked?" The internal temperature of the meat is the best most reliable way of knowing when your food is ready, whether you are cooking in a smoker or your kitchen oven. You can use a standard meat thermometer or if you like the idea of sitting back and letting your thermometer do the work use a digital thermometer with a probe on the end of a wire. You insert the probe into your meat, pass the end of the wire through the door of the oven, close the door, set the required temp for the type of meat and the thermometer will ring an alarm when your food is ready.

WOOD

Another question often asked is "What wood should be used?". These days there is the choice of wood pellets or wood chips. Both are commercially available as food grade products or you can make your own but be sure to not use any treated woods or woods that may have any oils, like the sawdust from the use of a chainsaw. As far as choice goes, Hickory and Mesquite are great all rounders with the fruit & nut trees being most suitable for white meats. Pellets will last longer than wood chips and on average you would use approximately 1/3 of a cup of pellets to 1 cup of chips. The biggest mistake people make when smoking meats is adding too much smoke, one load in the beginning will do it in most cases as once your meat seals you are not going to get much more flavour into the flesh. A little goes a long way, for small pieces of meat use a couple of tablespoons of pellets up to 1/3 of a cup for a roast.

The strength of the smoke flavour is very much a personal preference so base your usage of pellets or wood to your likes or dislike.

RECIPES

With the Masterbuilt Smoker your cooking choices are not limited to smoked meats. Breads, cakes, casseroles, slow roasts and even drying fruits and vegetables are possible. Most of your current recipes can be adjusted to cooking in the Masterbuilt cooker.

The following recipes have been designed to make your life in retirement as much about the journey as the destination. Stress free cooking is a big part of that journey, we all enjoy uncomplicated cooking and the gentle slowness and simplicity of a set and forget Masterbuilt Electric Slow Cooking Smoker oven takes out the stress and urgency.

It doesn't get better than that…

SMOKING ON THE MOVE

The Misty Gully is a 240 volt powered smoker that while somewhat small in size—may not be suitable for many on the road. There are however, many smaller, portable smokers about that could be used.

Equally, smoking food and cryovacing will allow that food to last for up to a month under refrigeration.

SWEET SMOKED SALMON

PREPARATION TIME: 8 MINUTES

SMOKING TIME: 30 MINUTES

Ingredients

3 to 4 fresh salmon steaks with skin on
½ tsp fresh dill
½ tsp black pepper
2 lemons
1 onion, thinly sliced

Suggested wood for smoking

Alder

Method

1. Wash and pat dry the Salmon fillets, place skin down on baking sheet.
2. Mix dill and pepper together and sprinkle over fillets.
3. Slice one of the lemons thinly, completely cover the fillets with the sliced onion, then the lemon.
4. Sprinkle each of the fillets with the juice of the other lemon.
5. Place the baking sheet on the bottom rack in the pre heated smoker and cook for 30 minutes or until the meat flakes. Use one small handful of chips.

SMOKED TROUT OR SALMON DIP

Ingredients

1 x 275 gm smoked trout or salmon (skinned and boned)
2 tbs/30 mL lemon juice
4 tbs/60 mL single cream or cream cheese of your choice*
2 tbs of finely chopped chives
Ground black pepper
125 gm butter

Suggested wood for smoking

Alder

Method

1. Put the trout flesh in a food processor or chop up finely with a sharp knife.
2. Add the butter, lemon juice, cream and pepper and blitz in a food processor for 30 seconds or blend with a fork until smooth.
3. Can be served creamy or chunky. Chill before serving.

HINT:

You can use regular cream cheese, curd cheese, cottage cheese, ricotta, or any other cream cheese of your choice instead of cream.

SMOKED STUFFED SALMON

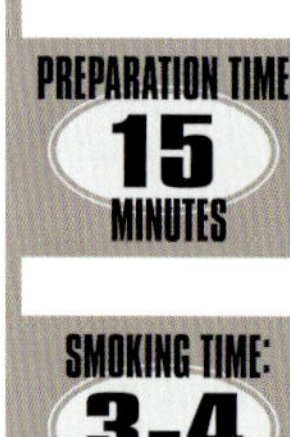

Ingredients

- 2 kg of whole salmon fillets
- 3 tbs oil
- ¼ cup spring onion (chopped)
- 1 cup tomato (peeled and chopped)
- ¼ cup dill (fresh and chopped)
- ½ cup bread cubes (dry)
- ¼ cup celery (chopped)
- ¼ tsp salt
- ½ tsp lemon pepper
- 1 clove garlic (minced)

Method

1. Prepare salmon and brush with oil.
2. Combine remaining ingredients.
3. Stuff salmon with mixture. You will need to be a little creative with the stuffing, slice the larger pieces vertically down but not all the way through, fill the centre and fold the sides over. The thinner tail ends can be sliced down the length and wrapped around themselves creating a pocket. You may need to use twine or toothpicks to help hold the steaks together.
4. Place salmon pockets on a sheet of heavy aluminum foil that has been doubled and greased.
5. Place in pre-heated smoker at 107°C and cook for about 3 to 4 hours. Smoke in the first 30 minutes.

Suggested wood for smoking

Hickory

SPICY CHICKEN RIBS

PREPARATION TIME: 10 MINUTES

SMOKING TIME: 65 MINUTES

Ingredients

2 1/2 tbs ground black pepper
1 tbs onion powder
1 tbs chilli powder
1 tbs garlic powder
1 tbs seasoned salt
2 kg chicken wings, rinsed and dried
1 cup honey
1/2 cup hot barbecue sauce
3 tbs apple juice

Suggested wood for smoking

Apple

Method

1. In a small bowl, mix together the black pepper, onion powder, chilli powder, garlic powder, and seasoned salt. Place the chicken wings in a large Ziplock bag. Pour in the dry rub and shake to coat the wings well. Marinate for at least 30 minutes (at room temperature) or as long as 24 hours (in the refrigerator).
2. Preheat smoker to 107°C. Place the wings on the top rack of the smoker and cook for 20 minutes. Turn wings and cook for another 25 minutes, or until internal temperature reaches 65°C.
3. While the wings are cooking, mix the honey, barbecue sauce, and apple juice together in a small saucepan. Cook over medium heat until warmed through. Remove the wings from the smoker and place in a disposable aluminum foil pan. Pour the warm sauce over the wings and toss to coat evenly. Return to smoker on second rack and cook for another 25 minutes, stirring occasionally.
4. Remove from the smoker and serve immediately.

HINT:

These wings are super spicy so use less dry rub or omit the Chilli powder for a milder flavor.

SMOKED TURKEY

PREPARATION TIME: 15 MINUTES

SMOKING TIME: 8-12 HOURS

Ingredients

- 5-6 kg turkey
- 1 tbs salt
- 2 tbs sugar
- 1 apple (cored, peeled, and quartered)
- 2 medium onions (quartered)
- 4 celery stalks with leaves

Suggested wood for smoking

Hickory or Apple

Method

1. Thaw turkey according to package directions if necessary. Remove giblets and neck. Rinse and pat dry. Sprinkle turkey cavity with salt.
2. Combine sugar and salt in small bowl. Dredge apple in mixture.
3. Stuff apple, onion and celery into cavity. Close with skewers.
4. Tie ends of legs to tail with kitchen string. Lift wing tips up and over the back to tuck under.
5. Preheat smoker to 107°C . Place turkey on middle rack and cook for about 8–12 hours or until inner thigh temperature reaches 82°C.
6. Remove from smoker and cover with foil, chill until needed or let stand 20 minutes before carving.

PORK RIBS

SMOKING TIME:
4-4.5
HOURS

Ingredients

- 1-2 kg pork ribs
- ½ tbs salt
- ¼ cup brown sugar
- 2½ tbs chilli powder
- 1½ tbs ground cumin
- 2 tsp cayenne pepper
- 2 tsp black pepper (freshly ground)
- 2 tsp garlic powder
- 2 tsp onion powder

Method

1. Mix ingredients and rub mixture on meat 2 hours before cooking. Allow meat to reach room temperature.
2. Cook ribs for 3 hours at 107°C in preheated smoker using hickory, one load, ½ cup at the beginning of the smoking period.
3. After 3 hours remove the ribs and wrap in heavy foil return to the smoker and cook for an additional 1–1½ hours.
4. Serve with your favourite BBQ sauce.

Suggested wood for smoking

Hickory

SMOKED PORK BUTT

Ingredients

3 kg leg or shoulder of pork
½ tsp salt
¼ cup brown sugar
2 tbs chilli powder

Method

1. Mix ingredients and rub onto pork butt.
2. Cook pork butt for 5 hours in 107°C degree pre heated smoker using apple wood chips during the first 3 hours.
3. After 5 hours remove butt and wrap in heavy foil. Cook for an additional 1 to 1 ½ hours. Internal temperature should be 70°C. Serve.

Suggested wood for smoking

Apple Chips

SMOKED LEG OF LAMB

Ingredients

- 4 cups apple or cherry wood chips
- 2-3 kg whole leg of lamb (with bone)
- ½ cup whipping cream
- 1 tbs Dijon-style mustard
- 1 tsp snipped fresh rosemary
- Cracked black pepper (optional)

Suggested wood for smoking

Apple or Cherry

Method

1. Trim excess fat from meat, pre heat the smoker to 107°C, place the roast on the middle shelf in the smoker.
2. Add chips to start and then another load after 2 hours.
3. Cook for around 6 hours then wrap in foil and continue to cook until the internal temp reaches 55°C, remove from the smoker and allow it to stand.
4. The temperature of the meat after standing should be 62°C for medium rare, and 70°C degrees for medium.
5. Meanwhile, in a small mixing bowl, beat whipping cream with a rotary beater or wire whisk until slightly thickened and starts to mound, stir in mustard and rosemary.
6. Serve immediately over lamb slices. If desired, sprinkle with pepper.

SMOKED SAUSAGE

Ingredients

Fresh pork or beef plain or flavoured sausage, Kransky's or Bratwurst are also cooked well in a slow cook smoker.

Method

1. Place sausage in pre-heated smoker at 100°C degrees.
2. Smoke until the sausage reaches an internal temperature of 68°C. Cooking sausages in the smoker at a low temperature eliminates the problems of splitting or over cooking.

Suggested wood for smoking

Hickory or Mesquite

SMOKED SCALLOPED POTATOES

Ingredients

4-6 potatoes (baking)
2 small sweet potatoes
1 purple salad onion
200 ml thickened cream
1 cup of grated tasty cheese
1 tsp garlic salt
Cracked black pepper to taste

Suggested wood for smoking

Hickory

Method

1. Wash and slice potatoes and onion into 1/4" slices.
2. Place in a shallow casserole dish layering vertically left to right alternating the potatoes and onion.
3. Mix the cream, garlic salt and pepper and pour evenly over the mix in the dish. Sprinkle the cheese over the top of the mix.
4. Place in the smoker on the bottom shelf for 1–2 hours or until the white potato is soft.
5. Start the smoke at the beginning of the time period only, approx 1/3 of a cup of chips.

SMOKED
CORN ON THE COB

PREPARATION TIME: 10 MINUTES

SMOKING TIME: 90 MINUTES

Ingredients

1 corn cob per person with husk still on
Soft or melted butter or oil spray
1 bunch green onions (finely chopped)
Salt
Pepper

Suggested wood for smoking

Hickory or Mesquite

Method

1. Prepare corn by gently pulling back the husks on each ear. Remove the silk but not the husks.
2. Place the ears in a large pan and fill with water to cover corn. Let soak for several hours. The water will soak into the corn cob and will steam the kernels from the inside.
3. Remove corn from water. Brush each ear with olive oil and coat with 1 to 2 tsp of chives. Salt & pepper to taste.
4. Pull husks back over corn. Place corn with husks in 107°C smoker for about 1½ hours.
5. Serve with or without husks. Remove husks to eat.

SMOKED SUMMER VEGETABLES WITH GNOCCHI

PREPARATION TIME: 20 MINUTES

SMOKING TIME: 60 MINUTES

Ingredients

Summer squash
Zucchini
Onion
Mushrooms
Cherry tomatoes
Baby spinach leaves
Crushed garlic
Parmesan cheese
Salt & pepper and herbs to taste
400 gm of fresh gnocchi
Extra virgin olive oil

Method

1. Rinse and thinly slice squash, zucchini and onion. Mix all the vegetables together.
2. Place the mixed vegetables into a large shallow casserole dish or make a large flat bottom boat using heavy foil.
3. Season to taste with your favorite herbs and spices.
4. Place the vegetables into the smoker at 120°C for 1 hour or until the vegetables are soft but firm, use ¼ cup of chips in the first 30 minutes.
5. Cook the gnocchi as per standard instructions, when all ingredients are ready gently toss together adding the olive oil, garlic and baby spinach leaves, sprinkle lightly with the Parmesan cheese.

Suggested wood for smoking

Hickory or Apple wood

SMOKED CABBAGE

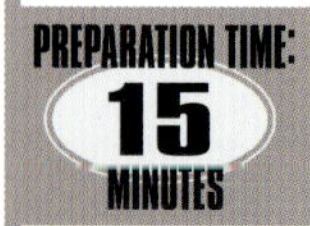

Ingredients

- 1 diced tomato, seeded and drained
- 3 tbs chopped onion
- 3 tbs chopped jalapeño
- 4 tbs Monterey jack or pepper jack
- 250 gm cheese shredded
- 1 stick unsalted butter, softened
- 1 tsp salt
- 1 tsp pepper
- 1 head green or red cabbage

Method

1. Load the wood tray with one small handful of presoaked wood chips and preheat the smoker to 107° C.
2. In a small bowl, mix tomatoes, chopped onion, jalapeño, cheese, butter, salt, and pepper. Set aside. Core cabbage, cutting out a good-sized cavity. (Make sure you do not core the base, leaving the cabbage open only at one end).Place the tomato mixture in the cavity and wrap cabbage with heavy-duty aluminum foil.
3. Place cabbage in smoker, cored end up, and smoke for 5 to 6 hours at 107° C .
4. Remove cabbage and discard foil and any blackened leaves. Cut the cabbage into wedges and serve.

HINT:

You can use either Savoy or red cabbage for this. Change it up by adding your own combinations of ingredients. Be sure to keep the top side up so the butter doesn't run out. You can leave a small opening in the top of the foil to allow for more smoke, but be aware that it's easily overpowered. Decide how much smoke you want, and adjust the opening to suit your taste. To test for readiness, squeeze it. If it's squishy, you're ready to roll. This is a great side dish to serve with ribs. Put it in the smoker along with the ribs and they'll both be ready at the same time.

FOUR-CHEESE SMOKED MAC'N CHEESE

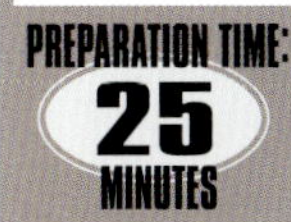

Ingredients

- 1 (450 gm) package elbow macaroni
- ¼ cup of butter
- ¼ cup all purpose flour
- 3 cups milk
- 1 (250 gm) cream cheese, cut into large chunks
- 1 tsp salt
- ½ tsp black pepper
- 2 cups (250 gm) extra sharp Cheddar cheese, shredded, and divided
- 2 cups (250 gm) Gouda cheese, shredded, and divided
- 1 cup (125 gm) Parmesan cheese, shredded

Method

1. Load the wood tray with one small handful of presoaked wood chips and preheat the smoker to 107° C.
2. Cook pasta in a large saucepan, filled with salted water, for 8 minutes or until al denté and drain. In a medium saucepan, melt butter and whisk flour into the butter. Cook over medium heat for 2 minutes, until bubbly and thickened. Whisk in milk and bring to a boil. Cook 5 minutes until thickened. Stir in cream cheese until mixture is smooth. Add salt and pepper.
3. In a large bowl, combine 1 cup cheddar, 1 cup Gouda, Parmesan cheese, pasta, and cream sauce. Spoon mixture into an 11-inch by 9-inch aluminum roasting pan coated with nonstick cooking spray. Sprinkle top with remaining Cheddar and Gouda cheeses.
4. Place in smoker and cook 1 hour at 107° C, until brown and bubbly.

HINT:

The smoke-infused flavor just adds an extra level to the old Mac 'n Cheese. If you are in a hurry, purchase ready-made mac 'n' cheese, top it with an extra layer of your favorite cheese.

SMOKED POTATO SALAD

PREPARATION TIME: 30 MINUTES

SMOKING TIME: 2 HOURS

Ingredients

700 gm russet potatoes, peeled
½ cup red onion, finely diced
½ cup pickles, chopped
3 hard boiled eggs, coarsely chopped
½ cup light mayonnaise
2 tbs cider vinegar
1 tbs Dijon mustard
Salt and black pepper

Suggested wood for smoking

Mesquite

Method

1. Load the wood tray with one small handful of presoaked wood chips and preheat the smoker to 107° C.
2. Peel potatoes and place them in a large saucepan with water to cover and boil for 20 minutes, until just tender. Drain potatoes, and dry them, on a plate layered with paper towels.
3. Place potatoes directly on the smoker racks and close smoker door. Reduce heat to 90° C and add more wood chips every 45 minutes. Keep potatoes in smoker for 2 hours. Remove potatoes from smoker and dice them for the salad.
4. In a large bowl mix onion, pickles, boiled eggs, mayonnaise, vinegar, mustard, salt, and pepper to taste. Add diced potatoes to the mixture, cover and chill salad in the refrigerator for several hours.

MUFFINS, CAKES & BREADS

No Wood chips required for Muffins and Cakes.

Choose your favourite pre mix from the supermarket or your favourite recipe and cook up your muffins or tea cake in the Masterbuilt smoker. They cook a lot slower than in your kitchen oven, allow approx twice the time as recommended. The result is the moistest Muffins or Cake that you have ever had. No more worries about them being cooked so fast that they end up burnt or dried out.

Prepare as the instructions outline using your standard cake tins and double the time for the finished product. Pre heat the smoker to 150° C.

You may like to try making a damper or Vienna loaf of bread with a light touch of smoke to give it that rustic taste.

Camp Ovens

Camp oven cooking has been around for perhaps two centuries in Australia. Europeans have for centuries been using heavy duty pots to stew up large quantities of food to prevent wasting.

Around the world the Aussie camp oven has a number of different names - Dutch oven (USA), Potjie's (South Africa), Tetsunabe (Japan) and Cocottes (France). Regardless of what they are called, camp ovens are renowned for creating unique flavours and textures in many food types. They share a unique place in Australian bush history with the early shearers and stockmen using these devices to cook their well earned meals. A few hundred years on and hardy travellers continue to enjoy the qualities of food prepared in the trusty camp oven.

Camp Oven Construction

There are several materials used to construct a camp oven these days. You will find cast iron and spun steel ovens as well as a few aluminium models making their way on to the market place. The variable construction of the different types of camp oven each carries a few pros and cons.

The original camp ovens were made from cast iron and many hardened travellers still prefer cooking with this construction material. Cast iron camp ovens are associated with heavier travelling weights and the potential for breakage if dropped, but they still provide easier camp oven cooking in that the heavy duty construction, once heated provides a more even heat transfer to contained foods. One of the most popular quality cast iron camp ovens available is the Furphy brand. Cast iron camp ovens do require specialised care and maintenance, and because it is a porous material – require "seasoning" of the oven prior to use. Seasoning can be done for all camp ovens but is most important for cast iron models. This requires washing with warm water and then lining with oil prior to heating on moderate heat. An occasional wipe of built up oil will complete the process.

To make travelling with camp ovens an easier task, early stockmen from the Bedourie Station in Queensland developed the spun steel camp oven. Spun steel camp ovens are much lighter to carry and more resistant to breakage. However, many a traveler has burnt their scones because heat management is a tougher ask when cooking on camp ovens made from this material! Bedourie camp ovens require building hot coals up around the oven to the midpoint as well as placing of coals on top of the oven. This will create a similar heating scenario as produced in the heavier cast iron ovens. The Bedourie ovens are designed to ensure the lid fits over the sides of

FACT BOX

TIPS FOR MAINTAINING CONSISTENT COOKING HEAT

My bushtucker man taught me a broad rule of thumb when calculating approximate camp oven temperatures. Cooking involved ensuring that the bottom and top sections of the oven were covered by a good layer of coals/heat beads. Each palm sized coal or heat bead can be estimated to contribute 7 to 10 degrees celcius to the camp oven. If you are good at your methods you will quickly establish the relative heat of your camp ovens relative to your home based conventional oven.

Effective cooking with the camp oven requires central positioning of the oven to ensure even heat supply. Ensure your heat source is not affected by wind or other sources of uneven cooling. Turning your oven a quarter cycle every quarter of an hour to maintain even heating. A handy tip when using heat beads includes covering the beads with aluminium foil that has the shiny side facing the oven.

the oven. This prevents coals ending up in your food and also has use as a fry pan when required. Other brands of spun steel camp oven include the Hillbilly and Aussie camp ovens.

When buying a camp oven you will see various sizes and geometries. Aim to buy a quality oven that will survive your travels and provide the quantities you expect to be preparing. Various models will have lids that can be used for other purposes and legs to allow convectional style heating from beneath.

Cooking on a Camp Oven

Camp oven cooking is often associated with some level of difficulty that sees many travellers shy away from using these wonderful tools. With a little patience and experimentation you will find yourself cooking some amazing meals if you are prepared to give camp ovens some time!

Cooking with Fire

To provide your cooking energy, an open fire or the use of heat beads are typically engaged to carry out camp oven style cooking. One of the really enjoyable parts of cooking on the road is using an open fire to carry out daily duties. Although not an essential part of camp oven cooking, an open fire adds that something special to the on the on-the-road experience. The fire aspect inspires feelings of the "old days" of evolution and seems to bring us that little bit closer to nature and our primeval roots. Information on developing the optimal fire is covered in our chapter on BBQ and Grills.

In the event that fire is not a valid option for cooking with your camp oven, other heating sources such as electrical plates and BBQ's can be used. BBQ's make for an easy and reliable method of heating heat beads for use with your camp oven. In the event of fire bans or soggy matches—you might have to settle for such a Plan B!

Pre heating a camp oven is a recognised part of the camp oven cooking proccss. Allowing a camp oven to heat in a controlled manner will ensure your oven does not contain hot spots when it comes to cooking time! Pre heating a camp oven can be done by sitting the oven next to a heat source to slowly heat the oven. You don't want the oven excessively heated during the pre heat stage.

Control and direction of heat supply are important aspects of cooking with camp ovens. Many meals are degraded through poor control and misunderstanding of the heating aspects of the camp oven. Being that food requires cooking in a nature similar to that of a conventional oven, heat must be applied from around (above and below) the camp oven. In the event that stews and liquid food types are being used in cooking, the camp oven may only require heat to be applied from beneath the camp oven.

I learnt some of the art of cooking on a camp oven from a cook that resided in Louth—western NSW. Locals referred to him as the local "bushtucker man" and he taught me that the key and by far hardest aspect of camp oven cooking was in judging the heat of your coals and exactly when it was time to cook—a learning developed from experience!

BUBBLE & SQUEAK SOUP WITH KANGAROO TAIL

Ingredients

Any vegetables that you have including
- Potato
- Peas
- Pumpkin
- Onions
- Carrot etc

5 Joints of a Kangaroo Tail
100 gm of Bacon pieces
1 cup of green split peas
½ tsp of Paprika
Salt and Black Pepper to taste

Method

1. Place the tail into a large camp oven add a pinch of salt and cover with water, boil for 2½ hours.
2. Add the rest of the ingredients including the diced vegetables and cook until they soften approx 1 hour.
3. Serve with a nice crusty damper.

TUNA POTATO PIE

PREPARATION TIME: 10 MINUTES

COOKING TIME: 45 MINUTES

Ingredients

800 gm canned tuna
2 tbs oil
2 onions, chopped
750 gm potatoes
Salt and pepper to taste
1 cup grated tasty cheese

SAUCE

1 cup milk
Pinch ground mace
1 stick celery
1 bay leaf
1 tsp whole black peppercorns
1 small onion, sliced
1½ tbs butter
1 tbs flour
Salt and pepper to taste
Fresh nutmeg
1 tbs wholegrain mustard

Method to prepare sauce

1. In a pan slowly heat the milk with mace, celery, bay leaf, onion and peppercorns until first bubbles form. Then remove from heat and let stand for 20–30 minutes.
2. Strain milk into a bowl.
3. In original pot melt butter and stir in flour over a low heat about 1 minute until mixture is smooth and just changes colour.
4. Remove from heat and slowly add milk until mixed through and smooth. (if lumps form and can't be removed, put the mixture through a strainer.)
5. Return to heat, stirring continually bring to boil and simmer for 5 minutes.
6. Season with salt, pepper, nutmeg and mustard.

Method for pie

1. In camp oven or baking dish heat oil and add onions.
2. Drain tuna and add to oven. Add freshly prepared sauce. Mix gently, cover and allow to cool.
3. Boil potatoes for 20 minutes. Pour off water, leave for 5 minutes until all water has evaporated. Mash potatoes with milk, butter, salt and pepper until smooth.
4. Spread potato over tuna / tomato mixture. Spread grated cheese over the top. Cover and bake for 25–30 minutes until cheese is golden.

CHICKEN CACCIATORE

PREPARATION TIME: 15 MINUTES

COOKING TIME: 60 MINUTES

Ingredients

3 tbs olive oil
6 chicken drumsticks
6 chicken thighs
1 large onion, chopped
2 celery sticks, chopped
2 carrots, peeled, chopped
150 gm sliced pancetta, chopped
3 garlic cloves, crushed
125 gm button mushrooms, sliced
100 mL dry white wine
800 g can diced tomatoes
½ tsp brown sugar
1 tbs balsamic vinegar
1 tbs chopped fresh rosemary
1 bay leaf
150 mL chicken stock
1 cup pitted Kalamata olives
Chopped parsley

Method

1. Heat the oil in camp oven over medium-hot heat. Add chicken and brown all over. Set aside.
2. Reduce heat to low. Add onion, celery, carrot and pancetta to the pan and cook for 5 minutes until the onion softens. Add the garlic and mushrooms and cook for a further minute.
3. Return chicken pieces to the pan, add the wine and simmer 1–2 minutes.
4. Add the tomatoes, sugar, vinegar, herbs and stock. Allow to boil, then reduce heat to low, cover and cook for 20 minutes, stir occasionally. Add the olives and cook for a further 10 minutes.
5. Transfer chicken to a heat proof dish, then reduce the sauce over high heat for 5–6 minutes
6. Serve garnished with the parsley.

CHICKEN HOTPOT

PREPARATION TIME: 20 MINUTES

COOKING TIME: 90 MINUTES

Ingredients

- 6 chicken pieces (serving sized)
- 4 tbs olive oil
- 4 rashers bacon, chopped
- 2 medium onions, sliced 1 cm thick
- 1 clove garlic, crushed and chopped.
- 3 medium carrots, sliced 1 cm thick
- 3 large mushrooms sliced chunky
- 2 sweet potatoes, sliced 1 cm thick
- 2 sticks celery, sliced
- 250 mL chick peas
- Rind of 1 lemon grated
- ½ tsp nutmeg
- ½ tsp thyme
- 750 mL chicken stock
- 250 mL white wine
- ½ cup freshly chopped parsley or 2 tbs dry

Method

1. Add oil to camp oven, bring to medium-hot and brown chicken pieces all over. Then remove chicken..
2. Add bacon and fry for 2 minutes.
3. Add onions and fry for 2 minutes.
4. Add garlic and fry for 1 minute.
5. Add carrots, sweet potatoes, celery, chick peas, lemon rind, nutmeg, thyme and brown.
6. Add chicken, mushrooms, chicken stock and white wine. Stir, cover and cook for 1 hour.
7. Remove lid and reduce liquid level if necessary, stir through parsley.

LOIN OF PORK
WITH TOMATO PESTO AND APPLE STUFFING

PREPARATION TIME: 15 MINUTES

COOKING TIME: 2–3 HOURS

Ingredients

1½–2 kg boned loin of pork with flap on and rind removed
1 tbs tomato pesto
1 tsb Honey Glaze (pp 61)
Chilli powder to taste

TOMATO PESTO AND APPLE STUFFING

1 cup soft white breadcrumbs
2 tbs tomato pesto
1 eating apple, finely diced
1 tbs honey glaze
salt, pepper
Chilli powder to taste

Method

1. Score the pork's fat layer in a diamond pattern with a sharp knife.
2. Mix stuffing ingredients together and place along the roast, where the flap meets the loin, roll and tie firmly with cooking string.
3. Rub the tomato pesto over the surface of the rolled roast.
4. Place in pre-heated camp oven and brown all over, with lid on in the coals of the fire, turning every 15 minutes.
5. Cook approximately 1 hour. Then brush with marinade, wrap in foil and cook for a further 1 hour.
6. Allow to stand before serving.

BEEF CURRY

PREPARATION TIME: 10 MINUTES

COOKING TIME: 1¾ HOURS

Ingredients

2 onions, sliced
2 tbs oil
1 clove garlic
75 mL water or stock
1 kg braising steak, diced 3 cm cubes
100 mL yoghurt
1 jar mild curry paste

Method

1. Heat camp oven to medium heat. Brown beef cubes on all sides, about 5 minutes. Remove beef.
2. Add onions and fry 5 minutes. Add garlic cook 2 minutes.
3. Add water and curry paste. Cook 1 minute, stirring.
4. Add yoghurt, stir. (Reserve some for topping)
5. Add beef. Cover cook slowly for 1–1½ hours.
6. Check occasionally. If it is too dry add more water.
7. Serve with rice.

BEEF STEW

PREPARATION TIME: 15 MINUTES

COOKING TIME: 1 3/4 HOURS

Ingredients

1 kg diced braising steak (2 cm cubes)
4 tbs oil
2 large onions, roughly chopped
2 cloves garlic, crushed and chopped
2 large carrots, roughly chopped
2 sticks celery, roughly chopped
1 tsp mixed herbs
1 bay leaf
Grated lemon rind
1 cup gravy or beef stock
400 mL dry red wine
Salt and pepper to taste

Method

1. Heat 2 tbs oil in camp oven, add onion cook 2 minutes then add garlic, carrots and celery cook further 10 minutes. Then remove from pan.
2. Heat remaining oil in oven and brown the diced steak in batches.
3. Return all meat, vegetables, mixed herbs, bay leaf, lemon rind and gravy then add salt and pepper to taste. Bring to boil then simmer for 1 hour then remove lid to reduce and thicken the sauce for 30 minutes. Check that the liquid level does not reduce too far.
4. Serve with boiled new potatoes.

BEEF STROGANOFF

Ingredients

750 gm braising steak
1 large onion, sliced
2 tbs oil
125 gm sliced mushrooms
2 cups gravy or beef stock
½ cup thickened cream (or sour cream)
2 tbs dry sherry
Salt and pepper

Method

1. Cup beef into thin strips.
2. Heat 1 tbs oil in camp oven. Brown meat in batches and remove.
3. Heat 1 tbs oil and add onion. Cook 3 minutes, add mushrooms and cook 2 minutes.
4. Add cream, gravy and sherry and mix well.
5. Add meat and mix well.
6. Cover and cook 30 minutes. Then remove lid and cook further 30 minutes until sauce reduces and thickens. Add more liquid if necessary.
7. Serve with rice or pasta.

SOY GLAZED BEEF EYE FILLET

PREPARATION TIME: 5 MINUTES

COOKING TIME: 60 MINUTES

Ingredients

1 whole beef eye fillet (about 1.2 kg)
3 tbs soy sauce
2 cloves garlic, finely chopped
2 tbs olive oil
Pepper to taste

Method

1. Remove all sinew and fat from eye fillet.
2. Mix remaining ingredients and place in a freezer bag with eye fillet. Tie bag and leave in refrigerator a minimum of 3 hours, preferably overnight.
3. Pre-heat camp oven and brown beef on all sides. Wrap in foil and return to camp oven. Cook for 25 minutes (rare) to 35 minutes (well done).
4. Remove from camp oven and allow to rest for 10 minutes before cutting into thick slices to serve.
5. Serve with a dollop of Bearnaise sauce and vegetables.

GOULASH

PREPARATION TIME: 20 MINUTES

COOKING TIME: $1^{3}/_{4}$ HOURS

Ingredients

- 1 kg braising steak
- 3 tbs oil
- 1 large onion, sliced
- 1 clove garlic
- ½ green capsicum, sliced
- ½ red capsicum, sliced
- 2 cups gravy or beef stock
- ½ cup red wine
- 450 gm tomatoes (or 1 can)
- 80 gm tomato paste
- 2 tsp paprika
- 500 gm waxy potatoes (desiree or similar)
- Salt and pepper
- Sour cream

Method

1. Cut steak into 2 cm cubes.
2. Heat 1 tbs oil in a camp oven to medium–hot and cook meat in batches until browned all over. Set aside.
3. Add capsicums and stir, then add gravy, red wine, tomatoes, tomato paste, paprika and salt and pepper to taste.
4. Cover and simmer for 1 hour then remove lid, check liquid level and cook uncovered for ½ hour to reduce it.
5. Serve on boiled/steamed potatoes and top with sour cream.

SHEPHERDS PIE

PREPARATION TIME: 10 MINUTES

COOKING TIME: 1 1/2 HOURS

Ingredients

750 gm coarsely minced beef
- 2 tbs oil
- 1 large onion chopped finely
- 1 tbs Worcestershire sauce
- 1 tbs light soy sauce
- 1 tbs mixed herbs
- 2 cups beef stock
- 1 tbs flour to thicken
- 1 kg peeled potatoes

Butter, oil or milk.
- 1 cup grated tasty cheese

Salt and pepper to taste.

Method

1. Heat camp oven to med–hot.
2. Add oil and onion, cook 5 minutes.
3. Add minced beef and cook until brown.
4. Add Worcestershire sauce, soy sauce and mixed herbs.
5. Mix flour with stock and add to oven. Bring to boil while stirring.
6. Reduce heat and simmer for 15–20 minutes as it reduces and thickens.
7. Boil potatoes for 20 minutes. Pour off water, leave for 5 minutes until all water has evaporated. Mash potatoes with milk, butter salt and pepper until smooth.
8. Spread potato over meat mixture. Spread grated cheese over the top. Cover and bake for 15–20 minutes until cheese is golden. You may choose to cook the pie in an aluminium disposable pan or a pie plate inside the camp oven. You may need to put coals on the lid of the oven to brown.

LAMB CURRY

Ingredients

1 kg lamb, diced 3 cm cubes
1 large onion, chopped
2 cloves garlic
3 cm fresh green ginger, finely chopped, or 1 tspn powdered ginger.
1 tsp cummin
1 tsp garam marsala
½ tbs mild curry powder
½ tbs hot curry powder
1 can tomato puree or juice
½ tsp mace
2 bay leaves
2 tbs oil
2 tbs fresh coriander, chopped
Salt and pepper

Method

1. Heat camp oven to medium heat. Brown lamb cubes on all sides, about 5 minutes. Remove lamb.
2. Add onions and fry 5 minutes. Add garlic, ginger, cumin, garam marsala and curry powder (you can vary the amount and mix of curry powders to your taste). Cook 2 minutes.
3. Add tomato puree and simmer 2 minutes, stirring
4. Add lamb and salt to taste.
5. After 1 hour check liquid level and add water or stock if the the meat is not covered by sauce.
6. Simmer for further ½–1 hour.
7. Serve with naan bread and turmeric infused basmati rice.

LAMB RACK
WITH PESTO

PREPARATION TIME: 15 MINUTES

COOKING TIME: 60 MINUTES

Ingredients

One rack of lamb with 3–4 cutlets per person
1 clove garlic, crushed
3 tbs basil, chopped
2 tbs Parmesan cheese, finely grated
Juice of half a lemon
2 tbs olive oil

Method

1. Trim fat from lamb racks (or use 'Frenched' racks).
2. Mix remaining ingredients into a damp paste. Add more wine and oil if necessary.
3. Make a slit between cutlets.
4. Rub paste over racks and into slits.
5. Brown racks in pre-heated camp oven. Wrap in foil and place in camp oven with lid on. Cook in medium coals for 1 hour. Remove and allow to rest.
6. Serve with salad or hot vegetables.

EASY PACKET POTATOES

PREPARATION TIME: 10 MINUTES

COOKING TIME: 30 MINUTES

Ingredients

- 2 medium potatoes, cubed
- 1 small Spanish onion, chopped
- 2 slices of bacon, chopped
- 1 tbs of whole grain mustard
- Grated Parmesan cheese
- 1 sprig of rosemary
- Salt and pepper to taste
- Aluminium foil
- Oil

Method

1. Add the mustard to the potatoes and onion and toss to get an even coating.
2. Oil two pieces of foil approx 30 cm x 30 cm and place the potato mix in the middle of both.
3. Divide the chopped bacon and add to the two parcels on top of the potato.
4. Sprinkle with a little Parmesan and add the sprig of rosemary, salt and pepper to taste.
5. Wrap loosely and tuck both ends upwards like a parcel.
6. Then place inside a camp oven with the lid on and cook for around 25–30 minutes, turn them over at 15 minutes.
7. These parcels can be prepared in advance and kept in the refrigerator until they are needed to be cooked. Experiment with a variety of vegetables.

STICKY TOFFEE PUDDING

PREPARATION TIME: 20 MINUTES

COOKING TIME: 30 MINUTES

Ingredients

170 gm dates, pitted and chopped
1 tsp bicarbonate of soda
1 cup boiling water
60 gm butter
170 gm castor sugar
2 eggs
170 gm self-raising flour
½ tsp vanilla essence

TOFFEE SAUCE

150 gm brown sugar
150 mL cream
½ tsp vanilla essence
50 gm butter

Method

1. Mix dates and bicarbonate of soda. Pour 1 cup of boiling water over dates and leave to stand.
2. Cream butter and sugar until pale. Add eggs one at a time, beating well after each addition.
3. Fold in flour, then stir in date mixture and vanilla.
4. Pour into a well buttered cake tin.
5. Place cake tin into camp oven at moderate heat 30–40 minutes until an inserted skewer comes out clean.
6. Serve with icecream and plenty of toffee sauce.

Method for Toffee Sauce

1. Combine all ingredients in a saucepan and bring to boil. Simmer for 5 minutes then remove from heat.
2. Re-heat to serve.

BREAD PUDDING
OR FAUX BOILED XMAS PUDDING

PREPARATION TIME: 15 MINUTES

COOKING TIME: 30 MINUTES

Ingredients

- 20 slices stale bread
- 500 mL orange juice or mandarin juice
- 2 eggs
- 60 gm brown sugar
- 2/3 cup of mixed fruit with glace cherries
- 60 mL brandy or rum
- 1 tsp cinnamon
- 1 tsp allspice
- 1 tbs melted butter
- 1/3 cup S/R flour
- Butter (extra)

Method

1. Remove crusts from bread.
2. Soak bread in orange juice until soft and mushy.
3. Separate eggs
4. Mash bread mixture and beat in egg yolks. Add sugar, raisins, mixed peel, brandy, cinnamon, allspice, flour and melted butter. Make sure it is really well mixed and mushy, if you have time put it in the fridge for a couple of hours to allow the brandy to soak into the fruit.
5. Beat egg whites until stiff and fold through the bread mixture.
6. Butter and flour the camp oven and pour the mixture in
7. Cook in camp oven on very low heat for 30–40 minutes until brown on top. Can be cooked on a gas burner. Don't be tempted to turn up the heat as it will burn the bottom of the pudding. You will get quite a bit of moisture under the lid, that is ok as this helps with the boiled pudding effect..

GENEVA PUDDING

PREPARATION TIME: 10 MINUTES

COOKING TIME: 30 MINUTES

Ingredients

175 gm Aborio rice
1.0 L milk
pinch salt
180 gm sugar
6 cooking apples
60 gm butter
½ tsp cinnamon
30 mL water

Method

1. Peel, core and chop the apples and place them with the butter, cinnamon, water and 30 gm of sugar in a saucepan. Cook until well stewed and mushy. Add remainder of sugar and allow to cool.
2. Wash and drain the rice, place it in a pan with 1 litre of milk and two pinches of salt. Cook until tender, adding more milk as required, and add sugar (about 60 gm) to your taste.
3. Butter your camp oven or ovenproof baking dish, Arrange the rice and apple puree in alternate layers, letting rice form the bottom and top layers. The rice will spread more easily if done when hot. You can also add a handful of mixed dried fruit to the rice for added flavour.
4. Dot with butter and bake at a moderate heat for 30–40 minutes until golden brown.

DAMPER

PREPARATION TIME: 5 MINUTES

COOKING TIME: 30 MINUTES

Ingredients

450 gm self-raising flour
1 tsp salt
15 gm butter
250 mL milk
125 mL water

Method

1. Mix flour and salt. Rub in butter.
2. Mix water and milk.
3. Make a well in the dry mixture and pour in milk mixture.
4. Mix until a firm dough is formed.
5. Place onto a floured board and knead until smooth.
6. Form into a round loaf and place into a medium-hot camp oven on oiled and floured foil.
7. Place extra coals onto top of oven so that top of damper browns.
8. Bake for 30–40 minutes until tapped damper sounds hollow.

Index

No matter where you are, ARB has you covered.

VICTORIA

ARB STORES

Head Office
ARB Kilsyth
42-44 Garden Street
Kilsyth VIC 3137
Tel: (03) 9761 6622

ARB Bairnsdale
623 Princes Highway
Bairnsdale VIC 3875
Tel: (03) 5152 1226

ARB Ballarat
891 Latrobe Street
Delacombe VIC 3356
Tel: (03) 5336 4605

ARB Bendigo
17-21 Phillips Drive
Kangaroo Flat VIC 3555
Tel: (03) 5445 7100

ARB Brighton
793 Nepean Highway
Bentleigh VIC 3204
Tel: (03) 9557 1888

ARB Dandenong
4A/6 Lonsdale Street
Dandenong VIC 3175
Tel: (03) 9793 0002

ARB Echuca
89A Ogilvie Avenue
Echuca VIC 3564
Tel: (03) 5840 2600

ARB Geelong
304 Thompson Road
North Geelong VIC 3215
Tel: (03) 5272 2611

ARB Hoppers Crossing
73-79 Old Geelong Road
Hoppers Crossing VIC 3029
Tel: (03) 9749 5905

ARB Keilor Park
34 Commercial Place
Keilor East VIC 3033
Tel: (03) 9331 7333

ARB Pakenham
20 Commercial Drive
Pakenham VIC 3810
Tel: (03) 5940 5500

ARB Shepparton
180 Benalla Road
Shepparton VIC 3630
Tel: (03) 5822 1877

ARB Somerton
798 Cooper Street
Somerton VIC 3074
Tel: (03) 9460 9988

ARB Traralgon
351 Princes Highway
Traralgon East VIC 3844
Tel: (03) 5174 9190

ARB Warragul
10 Howitt Street
Warragul VIC 3820
Tel: (03) 5623 5599

ARB STOCKISTS

Gippsland 4WD Centre
Lot 7 Princes Highway
Traralgon VIC 3844
Tel: (03) 5174 1560

Highcountry Parts & 4×4
201 Mt Buller Road
Mansfield VIC 3722
Tel: (03) 5779 1900

Horsham Off Road
72 McPherson Road
Horsham VIC 3400
Tel: (03) 5381 1766

Mildura 4WD Accessories
55 Seventh Street
East Mildura VIC 3500
Tel: (03) 5021 3213

Myrtleford Tyre & Battery
73 Myrtle Street
Myrtleford VIC 3737
Tel: (03) 5752 1175

Outback 4WD
174 Canterbury Road
Bayswater VIC 3153
Tel: (03) 9720 6226

Sale 4WD Centre
21-23 Union Street
Sale VIC 3850
Tel: (03) 5144 7990

SG Offroad Leongatha
2 Tilson Court
Leongatha VIC 3953
Tel: (03) 5662 5554

SG Offroad Wonthaggi
136 McKenzie Street
Wonthaggi VIC 3995
Tel: (03) 5672 5899

South Eastern 4WD Centre
182 Centre Road
Narre Warren VIC 3805
Tel: (03) 8786 5090

Swan Hill Off Road
1 Nyah Road
Swan Hill VIC 3585
Tel: (03) 5032 2700

Wangaratta 4WD Centre
205 Tone Road
Wangaratta VIC 3677
Tel: (03) 5722 2979

Warrnambool Offroad
1117 Raglan Parade
Warrnambool VIC 3280
Tel: (03) 5561 4354

Yarra Valley 4WD
35 Maroondah Highway
Healesville VIC 3777
Tel: (03) 5962 3124

WESTERN AUSTRALIA

ARB STORES

ARB Bunbury
2/12 George Street
Bunbury WA 6230
Tel: (08) 9721 2099

ARB Canning Vale
77 Bannister Road
Canning Vale WA 6155
Tel: (08) 9455 4366

ARB Geraldton
78 North West
Coastal Hwy
Geraldton WA 6530
Tel: (08) 9921 8077

ARB Mandurah
69 Gordon Road
Mandurah WA 6210
Tel: (08) 9583 3200

ARB Osborne Park
66 Collingwood Street
Osborne Park WA 6017
Tel: (08) 9244 3553

ARB South Hedland
2 Hamilton Road
South Hedland WA 6722
Tel: (08) 9160 4900

ARB Wangara
11 Buckingham Drive
Wangara WA 6065
Tel: (08) 9409 5764

ARB Welshpool
143 Welshpool Road
Welshpool WA 6106
Tel: (08) 9358 3688

ARB STOCKISTS

Action 4WD
19 Gillam Drive
Kelmscott WA 6111
Tel: (08) 9390 3011

Adventure 4×4
3 Crocker St
Rockingham WA 6168
Tel: (08) 9529 2229

Albany 4WD & Camping Centre
6 Minna Street
Albany WA 6331
Tel: (08) 6819 7777

All 4×4 Services
63 Strelly Street
Busselton WA 6280
Tel: (08) 9754 8588

Avon 4 Wheel Drive Centre
20 Peel Terrace
Northam WA 6401
Tel: (08) 9622 5818

Derby 4×4 and Marine
Lot 920 Wells Street
Derby WA 6728
Tel: (08) 9193 1919

Falcon Auto Parts & Accessories
Unit 17 651-669
Old Coast Rd
Falcon WA 6210
Tel: (08) 9534 6722

Kununurra 4WD Spares
21 Konkerberry Dr
Kununurra WA 6743
Tel: (08) 9169 1150

Make Tracks
44 Elgee Road
Midland WA 6056
Tel: (08) 9374 0777

Minshull Mechanical Repairs
96 Guy Street
Broome WA 6725
Tel: (08) 9192 5326

North West 4×4
2 Coghlan Street
Broome WA 6725
Tel: (08) 9194 5600

Off Road Equipment Myaree
61 McCoy Street
Myaree WA 6154
Tel: (08) 9317 4900

Pilbara Motor Group
7 Crane Circle
Karratha WA 6714
Tel: (08) 9144 6500

Pilbara Motor Group - Newman
18 Pardoo Street
Newman WA 6753
Tel: (08) 9154 3600

Southern Suspension & 4WD Centre
53 Norseman Road
Esperance WA 6450
Tel: (08) 9072 0917

Traction 4WD
179 Boulder Road
South Kalgoorlie WA 6430

TASMANIA

ARB STORES

ARB Burnie
1A Edwardes Street
South Burnie TAS 7320
Tel: (03) 6431 4494

ARB Hobart
5-9 Florence Street
Moonah TAS 7009
Tel: (03) 6232 2333

ARB Launceston
48 Holbrook Street
Invermay TAS 7248
Tel: (03) 6331 4190

ARB STOCKISTS

North West Off Road
24 Kelcey Tier Road
Spreyton TAS 7310
Tel: (03) 6427 3266

SOUTH AUSTRALIA

ARB STORES

ARB Edwardstown
957 South Road
Melrose Park SA 5039
Tel: (08) 8293 3225

ARB Elizabeth
27 Elizabeth Way
Elizabeth SA 5112
Tel: (08) 8252 1599

ARB Morphett Vale
181-183 Main South Road
Morphett Vale SA 5162
Tel: (08) 8186 6101

ARB Regency Park
606-608 South Road
Regency Park SA 5010
Tel: (08) 8244 5001

ARB STOCKISTS

Adelaide Off Road
65-67 Nelson Street
Stepney SA 5069
Tel: (08) 8363 5999

Allin Towbars
175 Richmond Road
Richmond SA 5033
Tel: (08) 8352 5155

Drop Bear 4×4 & Leisure
6B Augusta Highway
Port Augusta SA 5700
Tel: (08) 8642 2322

Clare Valley 4×4
273 Main North Road
Clare SA 5453
Tel: (08) 8842 3113

Copper Triangle
2-4 Graves Street
Kadina SA 5554
Tel: (08) 8821 2402

Goeverywhere 4×4
509 North East Road
Gilles Plains SA 5086
Tel: (08) 8369 0999

Hoop's Auto & 4WD Centre
232 Renmark Avenue
Renmark SA 5341
Tel: (08) 8586 5519

Jacksons 4×4 Accessories
61 Chris Collins Court
Murray Bridge SA 5253
Tel: (08) 8532 2550

LMG Performance
11276 Augusta Highway
Warnertown SA 5540
Tel: (08) 8634 3118

Mount Barker 4×4 Centre
1 Mount Barker Road
Mount Barker SA 5250
Tel: (08) 8391 4391

Port Lincoln 4WD
28-30 Mortlock Terrace
Port Lincoln SA 5606
Tel: (08) 8682 2424

Trident Tyre Centre
16 McDonnell Street
Naracoorte SA 5271
Tel: (08) 8762 3744

Trident Tyre Services
16 Bay Road
Mt Gambier SA 5290
Tel: (08) 8725 7799

Victor Harbor 4WD Centre
20-24 Adelaide Road
Victor Harbor SA 5211
Tel: (08) 8552 2543

NORTHERN TERRITORY

ARB STORES

ARB Alice Springs
30 Stuart Highway
Alice Springs NT 0870
Tel: (08) 8953 0572

ARB Darwin
892 Stuart Highway
Pinelands NT 0828
Tel: (08) 8947 2262

ARB STOCKISTS

Gove Motors
Arnhem Road
Nhulunbuy NT 0880
Tel: (08) 8987 1911

L&S Offroad
16 Jessop Crs
Berrimah NT 0828
Tel: (08) 8947 4771

Palmerston 4WD Spares - 4WD Repair Center
33 Georgina Crescent
Palmerston NT 0830
Tel: (08) 8932 3233

RJ Motors Katherine
1833 Stuart Highway
Katherine NT 0850
Tel: (08) 8972 2269

ACT

ARB STORES

ARB Fyshwick
188-190 Gladstone Street
Fyshwick ACT 2609
Tel: (02) 6280 7475